Stackpole 21⁹⁵/13¹⁷

DATE DUE			
SE 12 '87			
JE -9 '89			

Hunting Fringeland Deer

Other Books by David Richey

Hunting
Fringeland Deer

David Richey

Drawings by Tom Beecham

Published by Outdoor Life Books
Distributed to the trade by Stackpole Books

Library of Congress Cataloging-in-Publication Data

Richey, David, 1939–
    Hunting fringeland deer.

    Includes index.
    1. Deer hunting.   I. Beecham, Tom.   II. Title.
III. Title: Fringeland deer.
SK301.R53   1986   799.2'77357   86-23463
ISBN 0-943822-86-6

Manufactured in the United States of America

Contents

Acknowledgments

This book is the culmination of some thirty years of deer hunting, during which time I've made many friends from whom I've learned about whitetails. They are:

Claude Pollington of Marion, Michigan, whose 1,500 acres of prime whitetail fringe-land have been my study ground. He has been an inspiration to me and many other hunters who live for deer season;

Roger Kerby, an accomplished whitetail hunter, who also is an extremely capable guide specializing in deer drives—the ones that work more often than they fail. Much of what I know about driving whitetails I learned from this man. I've shared countless deer camps with Kerby and believe he is one of North America's top hunters;

Lee Blahnik, one of Kerby's guides, who's forgotten more about whitetail deer and their habits than many hunters ever learn and who will give you the best place to sit on a deer drive simply because he likes to see someone down a nice buck;

Herb Boldt, the epitome of the hardboiled newspaperman, who hired me at The Detroit News. A great hunter, Herb can down a running deer with one shot;

Matt Pollington, Claude's 19-year-old son, who was a tongue-tied teenager when I first met him, just entering his first firearms season. Using lessons learned from his father, he killed the biggest buck at the Buck Pole Deer Camp;

Art LaHa of Winchester, Wisconsin, an expert trailer and a legend in his own time, who taught me a great deal about deer and deer hunting. His sidekick, Marge Engle, another expert trailer, never misses an overturned leaf or the tiniest berry of blood. When she spoors a deer it's only a matter of time before the hunter attaches his tag to a buck;

George Gardner, archery representative, a good hunting buddy who has helped me to keep up with bowhunting trends;

Other sportsmen and companies who have been helpful include Paul Jalon of Chrysler Motors, who manufactures the lethal Zonker broadhead; Bob Eastman of Game Tracker fame; Jean-Paul Bisson of Le Chateau Montebello in Montebello, Quebec; and John McKenzie, Max Donovan, Paul Mickey, Air Canada, Bear Archery, Browning Bows, Gary Todd of Pro Release, Canadian Government Office of Tourism, Tink Nathan of Safariland Hunting Corporation, and the many state and provincial public information officers who furnished data on whitetail deer.

A special thank you to Ginny Commander and the Harris Outdoor Group for permission to rewrite portions of several articles originally done for their group of deer hunting magazines. And the same to *Outdoor Life, Field & Stream, Sports Afield, The American Hunter* and countless other outdoor periodicals who have previously published some of the information contained in these pages.

My sons, Dave Jr. and Guy, deserve special thanks for being attentive students during deer-hunting lessons. They have proved to be competent hunters and woodsmen, and I'm proud of them.

Introduction

Make no mistake about it—North American whitetail deer are here to stay.

Statistics compiled by federal agencies and state wildlife biologists point out that whitetails are twenty-four times more plentiful today than a hundred years ago. The reason: fringeland, or edge cover as biologists prefer to call it. That's what this book is about.

Man created the best whitetail terrain when he began clearing land for agricultural plantings and building homes. After heavy timber was cut and farmland opened up, whitetail deer prospered.

Whitetail deer numbers reached a low point in the mid-1800s when huge timber stands, often covering countless miles in each state, stood proud and tall and afforded little whitetail cover or food. Timber companies began cutting the trees the way farmers level a standing cornfield, and when they finished and moved on, little remained of the former forest. What did remain were young and tender shoots which rapidly grew into second-growth timber, and this provided food for the few whitetails which had survived in deep forest cover. As more land was cleared, timber harvested and edge cover developed, whitetails thrived and their numbers doubled, tripled and quadrupled until now they are abundant in nearly every state and Canadian province. Michigan, where I live, is a good example: The state now holds over one million whitetails, and for the last several seasons, hunters have killed approximately 140,000 to 160,000 animals yearly with bow and arrow, muzzleloader, rifle or shotgun. This just isn't done year after year in areas where whitetail numbers are in jeopardy.

Sure, Michigan and many other states or provinces own their share of deep woods or heavily forested areas where whitetail numbers are low. These areas, however, represent only a minute portion of the state's land resources. The rest is *fringeland* which supports many deer. Fringeland, by mail survey to each state and province, is estimated to represent 50 to 95 percent of most states' land resources, and it's in these areas where most whitetail thrive.

What is fringeland? By my definition, fringeland is what many sportsmen would term farmland with open woodlots, acres of fields under cultivation, sparse clumps of heavy cover surrounded by fallow fields, and bits and pieces of heavy and sparse cover near a smorgasbord food source.

But fringeland is much more. It's abandoned apple orchards, drainage ditches traversing thick or thin cover, and winding two-tracks through second-growth lands. Fringeland is also clear-cuts near heavy forest, cattail marshes, wooded pocket covers, swales, abandoned railroad rights-of-way and tangled thickets. It's also rolling hills and fertile farmland—everything but deep forest.

However, fringeland will invariably be found near farmland. It may be strictly rural or somewhat suburban. Detroit, for instance, is Michigan's largest city with millions of residents, but it's not uncommon to see whitetail deer within fifteen minutes of my downtown office at *The Detroit News* where I work as the outdoor columnist.

The key to this book, and to hunting fringeland deer, is to remember these animals need a good food source—whether agricultural or wild—near heavy cover where they can hide or rest, raise fawns and exist without constant human contact.

This type of cover is far more common than many sportsmen believe. Look around, and you'll find the heaviest number of whitetail deer are found near areas where human population is heaviest. The reason is simple: Deer live where fringeland or edge areas are plentiful, and where they can wax fat on plentiful foodstuffs while remaining out of touch with humans on a daily basis.

Before writing this book, I polled every state and province, and I turned up some startling statistics. For instance: Sportsmen who hunt the following states may not have realized just how abundant fringeland was in their area. "Consider that most of the state is fringeland," states a Vermont game biologist. Kansas reports "95 percent of our deer habitat is fringeland." Illinois has a growing whitetail herd, and 95 percent of the state is fringeland while the balance is deep forest and federally owned.

Tennessee boasts only 40 percent fringeland, while nearby Delaware feels 70 percent of its huntable land offers this type of terrain. South Dakota figures 80 to 90 percent of its land east of the Missouri River falls within the definition of fringeland, and most is farmland. The results of the poll appear in Chapter 10. Suffice to say that fringeland hunting opportunities are at their peak in North America, and a knowledge of the habits of whitetail deer and how they react to hunting pressure is important to hunting success.

There are many ways to learn more about fringeland deer in each state or province. The easiest method is to develop a rapport with the local conservation officer or wildlife biologist in your area. Learn where the heaviest whitetail concentrations are found, what percentage of the local habitat is fringeland and use some of the specialized techniques listed in this book. Good luck!

David Richey
Buckley, Michigan

CHAPTER 1

Know Your Foods

The buck moved like a night-prowling tomcat looking for field mice. He would stop and start, and pause to look around or to check the air with quivering nostrils for a hint of human scent.

This deer was cautious; I'd been watching him from my ground blind as he fed in a cornfield. Twilight had switched from a promise to reality, and as darkness crept across the field with long purple shadows the buck stopped feeding on corn and moved to the next food site.

I wanted him in front of my blind, within rifle range. He stopped once at 50 yards, but was screened by low sumac. Then he moved closer as my heart leapfrogged into my throat. "Just a few more feet," I muttered to myself while urging him on. "Just take two more steps."

The buck headed for an abandoned apple orchard behind me. He'd fed on corn and now was going to top off the evening meal with a whitetail's version of apple pie.

I snugged the Weaver crosshairs low behind his near shoulder, and when everything looked right I squeezed the trigger of my Model 70 Winchester. The .264 Magnum with its 100-grain softpoint roared. When the dust settled the buck was down.

He wasn't a trophy with antlers spread like wheelbarrow handles, but the handsome eight-pointer I'd been watching for two weeks during the preceding bow season.

Big deal! The guy watches a buck for fourteen days and shoots it on opening day of firearms season. Some hunt!

Whoa! Let's hold up here for a moment. Sure, the buck had been scouted, and watched intensively. But more importantly, I had learned about his feeding habits. That's why I was hunting near the apple orchard. If you know deer foods, know where seasonal foods are located, and know when and where whitetails feed, you'll be well on your way to scoring on antlered venison in the fall.

Many hunters who bowhunt or gun whitetails in fringeland areas are dealing with farm-fed deer. We know deer eat corn, oats, rye, winter wheat and other farmland goodies, but very few know *when* deer have the appetite for these foodstuffs.

Fewer still are the hunters who know what wild foods fringeland whitetails eat in their state or province, and during which season these foods are consumed. A fringeland deer hunter worth his deer tag and blaze-orange hat will study whitetails, their habits, and learn when, where and how local deer eat and on what. Believe it or not, this key factor is ignored by 95 percent of North America's hunters.

And some sportsmen wonder why they never score on whitetails.

Dr. Reuben Trippensee, in Volume I of his two-book series, *Wildlife Management* (McGraw-Hill Book Co., New York) states: "White-tailed deer have been described rather aptly as 'random tip browsers plucking at a twig here and a leaf there in an apparently thoughtless and unsystematic manner.' "

How true, but there's more. Farm-grown crops are systematically eaten by whitetails in many areas. In some cases sportsmen have learned that farmland or fringeland whitetails will consume more of a farmer's crop than can be harvested, and this leads to crop-damage complaints and herd thinning by the landowner or state conservation agency.

Deer are reasonably catholic in their approach to crops or wild foods, and will eat almost anything. Consider the following wild foods consumed during winter months based on a sampling from widely scattered states: chestnut oak acorns, apple, dogwood, hazelnut, mountain laurel, dwarf sumac, blackberry, greenbrier and orchard grass from Ohio. New York counters with round-leaved dogwood, staghorn sumac, flowering dogwood, basswood, apple and witch hobble, while Massachusetts deer favor apple, dwarf raspberry, ground hemlock, hazel, wintergreen, red maple, black cherry, red oak and hemlock at certain times.

South Dakota deer flourish on foods not common east of the Mississippi River. Some winter delicacies consumed by whitetails in this western state include bearberry, ponderosa pine, buckbrush, Oregon grape, wild rose, serviceberry, bur oak and a great variety of unidentified weed species, states Dr. Trippensee's book.

Whitetails which live in North Carolina's Pisgah National Forest munch on basswood, chestnut, sourwood, flowering dogwood, striped maple, red oak, red maple, black locust, mountain pepper bush, wild grape, greenbrier, saw brier, witch hazel and fetterbush during the winter months when truck crops aren't available. The reason fringeland deer numbers have increased and whitetail numbers in deeply forested areas have decreased is because of the available natural food supply. Unlike humans who can grow their own food, deer cannot—the food has to grow naturally in the wild or the animals will subsist on someone's garden or crop lands ... or die.

It isn't common knowledge, but a 100-pound winter deer needs 4 to 7 pounds of food daily to exist, and once an animal loses over 30 percent of its weight the critter is ready for the boneyard. In Michigan (and other states) deer often yard up (herd together) during winter months. Many deer yards have been picked clean of wild foods by countless preceding generations.

A good deer hunter knows to check for whitetail tracks in a cornfield or other area where deer browse.

Three classifications of wild deer food exist—preferred, good, and no-good or "stuffing" foods. Examples of preferred Michigan foods are ground hemlock, white cedar, red osier dogwood and red maple. Good foods include hard maple, aspen, jack pine and white birch. Starvation foods include balsam, red oak, cherry, spruce, tag alder and tamarack.

Wild foods can and will sustain wild deer, but farm crops often do a better job during times of slim pickings. The list of home-growns is nearly endless once all states and Canadian provinces are considered, but be advised that alfalfa, apples, barley, beans, clover, corn, celery, cherries, grapes, oats, peas, rye, rye grass, sassafras, soybeans, strawberries, winter wheat and others constitute a large portion of a whitetail's diet in many fringeland areas. If someone grows it, a whitetail probably eats it and flourishes in the process.

It must be remembered that deer are not beggars who will dine at the table of anyone who'll serve them. Wild whitetails mix it up, and it's very common for deer to feed on natural foods while in heavy cover and then move into a farmer's field at dusk to eat whatever happens to be growing in the area.

Whitetail deer, wherever they live, are complex creatures. Knowing how they eat and how they grow will help you hunt them.

Every deer hunter wants to shoot a buck. Sure, arguments are in favor of thinning the deer herd in certain areas through an antlerless harvest of does and fawns, but many sportsmen still live for the day when an antlered buck walks into their sights.

Consider that from Day One a buck (or doe) has an accelerated growth rate, and the major portion of the food ingested during the first two years goes toward body growth. Bucks that eat well during this period generally will have good body growth and good antlers. Does that eat well deliver twin and sometimes triplet fawns.

But, it's bucks that most deer hunters are interested in and the above statement does not mean that antlers do not grow while the buck is gaining weight. Antler growth accompanies body growth, but body growth takes precedence over the building of large antlers. Antlers will grow on any male deer, but big antlers and big body growth walk hand in hand. If a deer is merely subsisting, antler growth is minimal.

A deer needs about 17 percent protein in its daily diet. A deer's diet requires about 0.45 pecent calcium and 0.35 percent phosphorous for a well regulated antler and body growth. Some bucks get it and some do not, and those animals that do not receive these trace minerals often have small antlers and are somewhat smaller in body structure than whitetails on better range.

Two time periods are important for whitetails, and especially for bucks of six months to 1½ years—April through September and December through March. The first period is when bucks are rebuilding body weight after a long winter or when new-born fawns are first putting on weight. Older bucks of breeding age must feed heavily now to carry them through the rut, and the better quality of food they eat, the more likely they will enter the rut with heavy antlers.

The second period is critical to a rutting-age whitetail. The animals may lose up to

When deer are in the velvet stage of antler growth, they need good food. Although more food goes to body growth than to antlers, at this time the antlers need more nourishment than usual.

30 percent of their total weight during the rut, and this weight must be replaced before winter becomes too severe. Some bucks never recover from the rut, and old bucks which have spread their seed through the local doe population over a period of two months may not be able to regain this lost weight and may perish during a severe winter in northern states.

It's long been thought that 1½-year-old bucks have spike antlers, and older white-tails have four or more points. Nothing could be further from the truth. A spike buck is an inferior animal, and may never have anything more than spikes unless the food values change. I've seen spikehorns which were 5½ years of age taken off poor range

5

conditions. Introduce good food high in protein and trace minerals into a spike's diet, and the following year the animal and its antlers will blossom like flowers after a summer rain.

A normal whitetail buck at 1½ years, on good range with good food, will have from four to eight points. Granted, a young deer may have spindly points and very little spread, but each year the animal lives the spread increases as does the diameter of each point on both antler beans.

However, an overpopulation of whitetails on any given range (especially if the buck-doe population is heavily weighted on the side of does) can lead to a year-by-year reduction in the size of antlers. Does will eat most of the available forage, and thereby reduce food possibilities for bucks in the area. The male deer may suffer a decrease in antler size from one year to the next if food is scarce.

Food on prime whitetail lands can support just so many deer. An overpopulation of whitetails on the summer and winter range can result in weakened animals and unnecessary winter kill. Deer should be managed for quality rather than quantity, but this management policy is lost on many state conservation agencies. If numbers of deer over quality of deer is what people want, and what state agencies wish, then the lands should be managed to produce more food of a better quality.

Fringeland deer hunters can use this food knowledge to their advantage, but it does require some legwork. Determine through local state conservation agencies which natural deer foods are consumed during each season, and determine which truck crops are favored during winter months. In Michigan deer seldom bother much with corn during summer or fall months, but a field of standing corn near a January yarding area after one week may look like a swarm of locusts had stopped to dine.

Simply stated, certain foods are consumed at certain times of year. The savvy deer hunter who uses his head can turn this knowledge into good fortune. Food preferences, and specific times when whitetails consume these foods, may indicate where whitetails will be found from one season to another.

Grouse hunters have known for years that what ruffed grouse eat will dictate where they will be found, but it seems few deer hunters share this feeling. They bop out into the woods, pick a spot "that looks good," and wait patiently for a whitetail buck to meander by within shooting range. It's like waiting for a suicide to happen.

This waiting at good spots may work on occasion in some areas, but it seldom produces bucks in rural or suburban fringeland areas. Those enviable guys who "always seem to shoot a buck—year after year" are the ones who know when and where bucks feed, and on what. They trust not to luck, but to skill combined with knowledge.

A case in point. One year I was bowhunting whitetails on state-owned land in northwestern Wisconsin, and acorn mast was plentiful. I had scouted the area, and on two occasions had watched a handsome six-point buck sneak across the two-track trail ahead of my car at midday. I suspected he was gobbling acorns, and backtracked him to a beautiful oak stand. One thick spruce stood like a sentinel at the edge of the oak grove, and a faint deer trail followed the edge. I felt the buck might use that trail to cross the

This buck sneaked across a two-track trail in front of me and gave me a clue the animals were feeding in the acorns. Knowing what deer eat helps in finding their feeding grounds.

road to water. Three choices were considered—hunt the food, hunt the trail or hunt near the water. Time was running out on this hunt; I had but one day left to hunt before the Wisconsin firearms season would open the following week. I couldn't come back for another hunt, and it was now or never.

The choice was easy: I'd hunt near the food source. That afternoon I hoisted my tree stand into the spruce and anchored it so it would offer a broadside shot if the buck fed past me the next day. I planned to return the next morning long before dawn in hopes of being in front of the buck.

I arrived far too early the next morning, and spent a cold and miserable six hours in the tree. My butt felt like a practice field for the Detroit Lions' place kicker, and I soon wearied of waiting.

Shortly after noon the buck materialized like a ghost. One minute the oak ridge was empty, and the next time I looked up he was head down and feeding my way at a distance of 40 yards. The wind was in my face, and unless I moved at the wrong moment I'd have a chance to dust him.

The buck fed for thirty minutes without seeming to move two steps, and I kept thinking he'd soon have his fill of acorns and head past me and across the road for water. No such luck.

He continued to feed, and then either ran out of acorns in that area or decided another location might offer better pickings. In short, he started moving slowly and fed toward me with unhurried steps.

The buck bent over to nibble more mast, and then swiveled his head around at some unheard sound. I suspected more deer, but used the opportunity to lift my bow off the tree limb and positioned myself for an unimpeded shot should the buck continue his present course.

He turned, seemed to bore holes through me with a direct gaze, looked over his shoulder again at other deer making their way through the oak grove, and then after satisfying himself that all was well began striding down the trail. I'd guessed right. He was heading for water, and was following the same trail I'd watched him cross before.

I allowed the buck to pass my tree stand at 15 yards before coming to full draw. The sight pin nestled behind his shoulder, and when his near front leg reached forward for another step I made a smooth release.

The Bear broadhead sliced through the buck and stuck 6 inches in the ground on the far side. The whitetail whirled, seemed to sag for a moment and then ran full tilt in the direction from which he'd come. He covered 75 yards, and folded up his tent in plain sight. It had been a clean kill, and later his nut-sweet chops and steaks were superb.

Luck? Maybe, but I prefer to think of it as knowledge combined with an average amount of skill. If I hadn't seen the buck cross the road I may never have found the food source, and without the food source I never would have shot the buck.

Mast such as acorns, beechnuts, chestnuts, hickory nuts and the like figure highly in a whitetail's diet. States with mild winter or very little snow often will have bucks, does and fawns feeding all winter on this food source. An Ohio buddy of mine kills a buck each year under the same oak tree, and he does it in January.

"Winter bucks will scratch through snow to get to acorns," Bob told me, "and you can almost see a horizontal browse line crossing the ground where deer have dug up nuts. It's a daily progression, and by the time that on-ground browse line gets near my tree I know it's time to go hunting. I watch the browse line daily, and never begin hunting until it reaches my treestand location."

His last buck, a big wide-beamed ten-pointer, was shot at midday from his favorite stand. Such tactics aren't luck, but knowledge of a deer's habits and what food it prefers to eat. He knew from past experience that whitetails would be feeding on mast, and knew from which direction they would appear and it was only a matter of time before his big buck would graze within range and offer a shot.

Now, many of us do not have distinct areas where bucks amble along like milk cows heading for the barn. Few sportsmen have spots where whitetails literally feed on acorns along a prescribed route, and eventually line themselves up for a close treestand shot. Most of us just are not privy to such made-to-order situations. However, we are God-given an average amount of gray matter between our ears. It's this ability to think, and to savvy out how, when and where whitetails will feed which makes man the supreme predator. This doesn't mean we score each time we go hunting. If such were the case we'd soon tire of hunting, and take up some mundane sport like racquetball or squash or sit home watching sleep robbers on television.

No, hunting appeals to us because it places a heavy premium on knowing something about the quarry, where it lives, how it reacts, what it feeds on and where it goes in times of danger. Humans, for all our brains, often commit errors in judgment which allow trophy whitetails to live long enough to instill big-deer genes in enough fertile does to perpetuate the species.

Sure, everyone knows what corn or soybeans look like, but if you were to transport this Yankee down South I may be hard put to identify mountain laurel, witch hazel or the other southern wild foods. Every state conservation agency will probably be willing to supply a courteous sportsman with a list of wild foods available in that area, and many will supply line drawings which illustrate what these wild foods look like. It's then up to you to learn these wild foods.

Your ability to become a proficient whitetail hunter rests solely on just how much you're willing to learn. These wild foods and truck crops can be learned overnight without pain or strain. Remember that truck-crop food sources may change from year to year in a specific locale, but a quick check in soft earth near each source will reveal whether whitetails are utilizing these foods. Learn when each food type is consumed by farmland deer, where the animals feed on wild foods, and where they bed and you'll be a leg up on other deer hunters.

Whitetail foods are important, but this knowledge is only one small portion of the deer-hunting riddle. But, agricultural and wild foods are two key pieces around which fringeland deer-hunting success is built and this information is needed to make the other subjects of this book fall into place.

CHAPTER 2

Know Your Terrain

It's a well-known fact that the best deer hunters are those who are intimately familiar with local whitetail terrain. They know where deer feed, where they bed, which routes they use to travel to and from bedding areas, and which escape routes they follow when danger threatens.

Learning these facts from reading them in a book is akin to finding out that publisher Rupert Murdoch has money. How the Australian newspaper magnate made his money is easy to learn, but learning how terrain differs is meaningless unless hunters are willing to lay down boot leather to learn the local terrain as one would learn the dimensions of a new house. Only time and experience can teach a deer hunter how to recognize excellent whitetail habitat at a glance.

The length and breadth of North America is a maze of differing terrains. Habitat where whitetails thrive in the Midwest is totally different from that commonly found in southern states. Western deer live in an environment different from whitetails in northern Minnesota, and terrain where whitetails may thrive in eastern Tennessee along the foothills of the Great Smoky Mountains will be far different from what Maine whitetail hunters might encounter.

The fringeland deer hunter must know his foods, and learn how to identify which type of forage is best for the season. But once that data is digested it must be pancaked together with a deer's terrain requirements—something like a ham and cheese sandwich for a hungry hunter.

One of the most important things I thought I once learned was told to me by an old codger years ago when deer hunting was but a glimmer of hope in my teenage mind. The oldtimer had shot a few deer, as I recall, but he didn't score each year and was seldom seen in the woods.

"Find yourse'f the highest hill in the area, and sit tight," the old coot said. "Them deer, why, they be crawlin' all over ya as soon as the opening-day guns go bang!"

"Oh, yeah," I asked. "Why's that?"

"Them deer will be leaving the co'nfields, and tryin' to get up high wheres they can watch the redcoats."

"No kidding? I always thought they headed for thick cover."

"Nosirree. They head up topside to keep a sharp lookout for hunters, and that's where ya should be sittin' with your shotgun. Get 'em when they come over the crest of the hill."

Amazing, I thought. Here was my chance to be the first kid on my block to whack out a deer, and the old man had felt enough pity for my scrawny soul to pass along his cherished words of wisdom.

Well, the opening-day guns went bang and I could see the redcoats. They were sitting in ground blinds near the "co'nfields," and they were shooting deer. Whitetails scooted in every direction, but if memory serves me correctly the scurrying deer seemed to be following a prescribed course toward safety . . . through heavy cover.

I didn't shoot a buck that year while sitting on the highest hill in the area, and I didn't take one the following year from the same spot. The oldtimer bad-mouthed me, and insinuated movement on my part must have spooked any bucks heading my way. The second year I didn't move a muscle, and that hilltop was about as dreary as a Russian love story and as devoid of whitetails as the Sahara desert. The only whitetails I saw that year looked about the size of a gnat's backside as they scrammed away from the hilltop. Oh, I saw a few bucks, but other fringeland deer hunters had them securely fastened to the roofs of their vehicles for the long drive home.

The second winter of my deer-hunting career was spent reading everything I could about the critters. I wanted to know when and where they fed, how and when they made babies, when their antlers grew and fell off, and every other little tidbit of data which could be obtained from what was then the Michigan Conservation Department. If published material was about whitetails and deer hunting, I tracked it down like Sherlock Holmes after one of the bad boys and devoured the information in throat-choking chunks.

I absorbed whitetail information like a new kitchen sponge absorbs water, and discarded worthless information such as the well-meaning oldtimer had offered. I learned that in some western states whitetail deer do go high and squirrel themselves back into secure corners where they can watch their backtrail and escape over the top without being seen. But I also discovered that fringeland whitetails—those deer found in or near rural or suburban locales where farm crops are a major part of their diet—seldom go high. Fringeland whitetails are masters at losing themselves in some of the thickest cover this side of a dense swamp or in areas where a hunter would least expect to find a deer. Since those early beginnings I've routed nice bucks from thickets no larger than a small brushpile, and I've bounced them from a low spot with high grass in rolling hills. They've been rousted from thick swamps an acre in size, cattail marshes and the like;

but one fact holds true wherever fringeland whitetails are found—they seldom head for high ground but instead hide out in areas where few hunters tread or wise men fear to go.

Of paramount importance to a fringeland deer hunter is to know the terrain. Topographical maps can be useful, but nothing can beat walking the area on foot. Some hunters I know will walk almost every inch of the proposed hunting area, and make their own map. They look for feeding and bedding areas, trails to and from those sites, and they minutely examine the terrain for buck sign such as rubs and ground scrapes. They know where bucks travel along an escape trail if the heat gets too great, and they learn the terrain from a hunter's viewpoint.

It is this knowledge of terrain on an intimate basis which separates men from boy hunters, as I can well testify from my dismal failure as a young nimrod. Good hunters know where preferred wild foods are located, and they know where truck crops will be found. If they can locate these foods, so can deer.

Only through thorough scouting of an area can a fringeland deer hunter learn enough of the terrain to make an accurate decision as to where whitetails will move. Deer begin moving, almost universally, about an hour before dusk from a bedding area to a location chosen for feeding. The reverse happens about an hour before sunup when deer begin moving along familiar trails back to the bedding area. It's along these trails where hunters hope to intercept deer.

Whether they do or don't depends, to a large degree, on how well they know the terrain. An area should be familiar to the hunter, and the sportsman should know it as well as the animal being hunted.

Fringeland areas are quite easy to scout, and to familiarize yourself with. They are far different from, say, huge cedar swamps or large forests. The farmland or fringeland areas may be small or large, but you must know where heavy cover is for a hunt to be a success.

Heavy cover may be a huge mile-square cornfield, or a railroad right-of-way. It can be a cattail marsh, sumac swale, abandoned fruit orchard grown over to briers and brambles, small (or fairly large) woodlots, drainage ditches, low brushy tangles in the middle of open fields or any other thick-cover area where deer can hide.

One important fact must be remembered about most fringeland deer, and it is that they'll seldom travel more than one mile to feed on any farm-grown crop. They may munch on wild goodies near the bedding area, and they may feed for days in such an area of plenty, but only rarely will they travel long distances to feed in a farmer's soy bean or winter wheat field.

Whitetails, like many humans we know, are basically lazy and seem reasonably content with their lot in life. If this fact is kept in mind we can better understand why a prime deer-bedding location may be found within 200 yards of a choice place to eat (if the foodstuff is acceptable to deer at that time of year). If local deer prefer to feed on buckwheat, for instance, and the nearest buckwheat patch is three miles away, they will

Topographical maps are a good guide to locating productive hunting areas. Of course, walking the terrain before deer season begins also helps.

look for a substitute (such as oats) closer to home if a choice of wild goodies is available to supplement the diet.

If the main forage crop during your hunting season is acorns, it wouldn't make sense to look for nearby bedding whitetails and the trails they use to and from bedding sites near a cornfield if visual observation discloses few fresh deer tracks at such sites. You must hunt near areas where deer feed on a daily basis.

The ability to match food and terrain can be learned—once you get the hang of it. Whitetail deer in fringeland country go where the best foods for the season are located near their bedding areas, and they follow certain terrain features to reach their objective. If we keep that thought foremost in mind it becomes the logical second step to examine certain types of fringeland terrain where whitetails are found.

Small rubs, such as the one on this big popple tree, and the ground scrape near the hunter's knee, are clues to the whereabouts of a big rub.

This hunter has found tracks in the soft earth, indicating deer are in the area.

100 Percent Farmland

In areas where farmland is plentiful very few locations remain which are 100 percent farmland. A mile-square cornfield with roads on all sides would certainly qualify, and deer can and will use such spots to satisfy their three basic needs—food, cover and water.

Take it from one who knows: trying to move a buck from a huge cornfield within bow or gun range is as much fun as a wrestling match with Man Mountain Dean. All you get is beat up, tired and hassled from the exertion, and the deer crawls under another corn row and gets away.

I remember a time we watched a tremendous buck slide across a dirt road and into a large cornfield at noon. The whitetail was so fat his belly jiggled like Jello, and his rack numbered at least twelve heavy points. It looked more like a hatrack, or the front end of a car after a head-on collision, than a set of antlers.

Larry Jacobson and Marv Whitcomb, two longtime hunting buddies, were with me. I figured that fat old boy would be a piece of cake.

"I'll take the track," I said. "You guys spread out, and one cut to the north and pick up a good game trail heading out from the corn and the other do the same on the east side. This guy doesn't have any cover on the south or west sides, and should head toward one of you."

How naive I was. Clueless would be a better description.

I took the buck's tracks through the snow after giving my friends fifteen minutes to work into position. The snow deadened my approach, and I ghosted along as quietly as a hunting owl.

The buck went into the corn only 50 yards, meandered back and forth through the rows a little bit and laid down. No, I didn't shoot him in his bed. He got up from his bed as I entered the corn, moved over several rows and continued to lead me in a circle for four hours.

I finally worked out of the corn to Jacobson, and asked: "Have you seen anything?"

"No, and Marv was down here an hour ago and he hasn't seen the buck. Where did he go?" he asked.

The truth was that without an army or several battalions of hunters it would have been impossible to move that buck from the huge cornfield. He stayed just far enough ahead of me to jump off to one side and backtrack a little ways. On several occasions I found where he stood 10 feet away and watched me blunder along his trail.

Darkness fell and we didn't get that buck, and we never saw him again. This points out, within reason, the futility of hunting an area which is mostly huge tracts of cropland.

We would have been much wiser if we had taken up positions along game trails as I should have suggested, and waited for the buck to show himself just before dark. But, we were certain he would bed down, and then run in panicked flight for heavy cover to the north or east. Instead, he did just the opposite and remained in the heaviest cover (the cornfield) and led me on a round-robin course which accomplished nothing except to tire me out.

Huge tracts of cropland as I've described will hold deer, but only in times of danger. Frequently, deer will bed down in nearby heavy cover and only venture to feed on corn at dusk.

The ideal situation would be to scout the immediate area and determine by which runways or trails deer enter and leave the cropland at feeding time. Look for deer trails to follow brushy fencerows, ditches which drain cropland, narrow fingers of woods which connect adjacent woodlots or any other terrain feature which affords cover during daylight periods.

A piece of land which is 100 percent farmland or cropland such as standing corn is difficult to hunt, even harder to move whitetails from and your chance of success is minimal. It's far better to consider where deer are going, where they are coming from, and try to catch them before they reach such heavy-cover areas.

Small Woodlots

Some of my fondest deer-hunting memories are of small woodlots. I'm talking about a type of terrain common wherever fringeland deer are found— a parcel of woods from 1 to 10 acres, and preferably longer than wide on the upwind side. Wind direction is very important to deer hunters, but the prevailing wind must coincide with the lay of the land or terrain features.

I like small woodlots; you know the kind, all grown over to briers and brambles which tear hell out of the fashion jeans and hunting pants alike. Often there are forgotten bits of timber and berry bushes . . . and at odd times, deer.

Many fringeland areas are posted. This makes it all the better for a deer hunter with trespass permission because whitetails often hole up where not every dude with a blaze-orange vest can hunt. Small woodlots are a prime example.

This type of terrain feature is common through the East, Midwest and South, and whitetails—especially big bucks—thrive in such locations. They have cover, access to nearby heavier cover and food if they wish. You can find such locations by pre-season scouting. All a deer hunter needs to know is how bucks (does are deer, too) travel into the area and how they leave it. Tracks in soft earth near croplands, signs of rubs or scrapes or other sign will indicate the presence of whitetails.

Look for woodlots which have some type of inside cover which leads to heavier cover. Again, a narrow finger of woods or drainage ditch which connect a small woodlot with a larger one is an ideal location for trophy deer.

John McKenzie, of Millington, Michigan, and I used to team up on deer in small woodlots, and we seldom went past the second day of Michigan's sixteen-day firearms season without hanging our tag on two nice bucks. We scouted them hard, worked out techniques (explained in a later chapter) and scored when deer decided the pressure was too hot in the kitchen and opted to move to an area with less traffic. One thing we learned is that many fringeland deer hunters bypass woodlots which are visible from side to side. They usually pass over an opportunity at some good bucks as well. We learned, early in the game, to allow brush busters to move deer to our select locations and we would shoot the bucks they hoped to find.

Wind direction is important in deer hunting, and it's doubly important when gunning whitetails in small woodlots. A puff of wind from the wrong quarter once blew a chance for a woodlot hunting buddy. He'd been on stand for two hours, and the wind was in his face and blowing from a nearby heavy cover where he expected deer to be holding. He was waiting downwind near another woodlot where the bucks were expected to head once opening day gunning pressure became intense.

"I'd been there for two hours, and any minute felt a buck would slip out of the bigger woodlot, cross the field into my woodlot and try to sneak out across the road into the big swamp," he said. "I sat tight, and several dudes tried a noisy drive on the big woods about 10 a.m. in hopes of pushing out an antlered deer.

"Five minutes later a buck slipped from heavy cover, ran along a fencerow for 100 yards and then dashed across an open field toward me. He entered my woodlot and two minutes later was moving my way, but was screened by thick brush 50 yards away.

"The wind had been in my face all morning, but once that buck closed the gap I felt the telltale cooling of my neck hairs and knew the game was over. That buck slammed to a stop, tested the wind and he knew exactly where I was posted. He vamoosed out one side of the tiny woodlot, and the last thing I saw was his tail disappearing over a fence 200 yards away. He never came back, and I'll never forgive that wind direction change. That bad wind cost me a big buck."

This anecdote points out a very important point; well, maybe even two, but the first is that fringeland deer are as savvy as whitetails anywhere and pay a great deal of attention to what their nose tells them. The second point is that deer will follow desired cover whenever possible, but will not think twice about abandoning a terrain route if danger is present and they feel threatened.

The best woodlots are those bordered on two or three sides by open fields, and those that have brush-choked fencerows leading into or out of heavier cover. Look for woodlots with tangles of heavy brush, briers, berry thickets or other heavy cover within, but don't overlook the nearby access to food and/or water. An ideal woodlot, in my opinion, will be 100 to 200 yards long and from 30 to 60 yards wide.

Choice wooded areas are here, there and everywhere in fringeland locations. They dot the countryside, and can be seen from main highways, back roads and two-track trails. Many are behind homes. They all have a common denominator. They almost always connect via a fencerow, thin finger of woods or some type of heavy cover with another woodlot. These hotspots are not big tracts of land, but are relatively small. Size means little when one judges it for deer habitat, but such areas will feature thick cover for the animals.

Ignore semi-clear-cut woods where hunters can see from side to side, or from end to end, and forget about those that border fallow fields or other lands which do not support food crops. Look for wooded locations with food on two or three sides where visibility (from inside) is good and where whitetails have an avenue or two which can be used for escape if danger threatens.

Opposite: An open field borders this southern woodlot, and the hunter is on target as whitetails move back into the brush after feeding.

Hill Country

My definition of fringeland deer habitat would have to include hilly or rolling terrain. Hill country offers exciting hunting possibilities, but it places an extra demand on sportsmen to know how, when and where whitetails travel to food or bedding areas.

If the area you hunt is hilly, and has farmland nearby, it probably qualifies. One important thing to remember: If the land is hilly, it has to have corresponding gulleys or ravines as well. One trick to recognizing and learning to hunt hill-country terrain is to know that untroubled deer often will cross open hillsides as a matter of course just as often as they follow the bottom or sides of a gulley. It's what they do during times of danger that may spell their downfall.

Many hills in fringeland country are rather open. Some may have copses of trees along the sides or on top, but open visibility is a key factor. If you can spot a buck moving 400 yards away it is likely he can spot you as well.

A haybale blind overlooking a hilly area is good, but the hunter must be there ahead of the deer.

Almost every hilly area I've hunted have one or more small depressions ringing the edge in which deer can travel without being spotted. Deer often travel along these minor ridges or gulleys during daylight hours although they will move through open areas under cover of darkness.

My old buddy, the one who stuck me on a hill as a teenager, was partially right about whitetails but not in the area he placed me. He figured deer would swarm around me like flies over road apples, but he guessed wrong in that location. He was on target where the terrain is almost entirely made up of hills, and where whitetails must travel or circumvent those hills to get from bedding to feeding sites and back again. My friend had both oars in the water, but not at the right time in the lands I hunted thirty years ago.

It's extremely important to locate hill country trails being used at dawn and dusk by whitetails. Look for droppings, hair caught on barbed-wire fences and tracks in low, wet spots. Learn where deer travel, and look for a nearby ambush spot. Another hill overlooking such areas affords superb locations for a pit blind, and since most of the hunter is below ground it can be a fine spot to waylay a buck on opening day. The trick is to find the proper location which overlooks trails being traveled by whitetails at a time when hunters are afield.

Hill country is fascinating hunting territory for fringeland deer, but a hunter must learn to see those areas where deer travel and know when they pass through. One of the best ways to collect a hill-country buck is to watch a specific location for a week or two prior to deer season and learn where deer travel. Be there ahead of the animals, and be ready. My Bushnell spotting scope has helped me locate moving animals many times in hill country, and a pair of binoculars, a rifle or a spotting scope can be an asset for any hunter.

Abandoned Farm Orchards

Fringeland bucks are not stupid, mildly crazy or weird. They survive by hanging out in some unorthodox locations, and these areas commonly will be places where few hunters tread.

An abandoned orchard growing up to tangles of forgotten berry bushes is a prime example. Many look like areas better noted for cottontail rabbits than deer, and this is one reason many sportsmen say, "Ah, the hell with it. It's too thick in there; we'll rip our clothes apart just looking for tracks."

Chances are good a buck was sitting tight within 50 yards, and listened to the hunters discuss the various reasons why they shouldn't hunt the cover. I've seen this scenario played many times, but a tangle where even an 11-inch beagle would find tough going is just the type of jungle frequented by fringeland bucks. These animals avoid humans, and going to ground in such locations is just one reason why they often grow the heaviest antlers and live longer than other deer. They are savvy, and know how to avoid human contact.

I hardly think an abandoned orchard can be too thick for a whitetail buck. I once saw a pretty eight-pointer jump a fence when hounded by hunters, and he jumped smack dab into an old orchard so thick two fleas would have had trouble trying to dance. The tangle was a mixture of blackberry and red raspberry bushes, and if you've ever tried walking through those jaspers you know what I mean. Even bird-shooting pants are ripped by the little briers, but the buck seemed to slide through the vines like he was coated with Dri-Slide or graphite. He hit the brambles, and didn't even slow down until he was 50 yards inside the fence and out of sight.

The hunters saw him go in, but there wasn't a man among the bunch with enough gumption to try rooting him out. Everyone thought he went through the orchard and out the other side, but it wasn't true . . . at least, not right then. He came out the opposite side two hours later, and nasty ol' Dave Richey was there to lower the boom. I simply figured if they wouldn't drive him out I would sit on the crossing on the downwind side and take him if he showed before dark. He did, and I did.

I didn't hunt that orchard, but I knew the buck would show sometime. Orchard fringes can be hunted, or on escape trails leading out, but if you hunt inside they can produce trophy fringeland bucks.

Drainage Ditches

The largest nontypical whitetail taken in Michigan as of this writing was shot by Paul Mickey of Kawkawlin in Bay County in 1976. It scored a tremendous 232 5/8 points according to the Boone & Crockett Club—a tremendous buck by anyone's standards. That, in itself, is rather amazing once you realize much of Bay County is as flat as my typing desk and is not known to be much of a deer-producing area. The other amazing thing is that Mickey had a previous chance at this big guy, and flubbed it.

He had spotted a buck feeding in an open field. At his approach along a drainage ditch the buck wheeled, jumped into the ditch and started running his way. Mickey saw what was happening, and when the massive buck was out of sight he jumped out of the ditch onto the tiny dike to nock an arrow on his bowstring. What Mickey didn't know was the buck also had left the ditch, and when the hunter came topside the heavy-antlered whitetail damn near ran him over in a head-on collision.

"That buck threw on the brakes," Mickey remembers, "and started skidding to a stop. I could have touched him with the tip of my bow, but I was too astonished to do anything but stare at those antlers. The buck wheeled and disappeared into the ditch. I didn't see him again for several weeks until I shot him with a rifle."

Paul Mickey has taken several Pope & Young record-book whitetails from Michigan, plus the one B&C buck. He hunts strictly for trophy deer. He believes, as I do, that

some monster bucks often call drainage ditches, creek bottoms or river flats home.

"Spots like this are seldom hunted by many hunters," Mickey said. "Many sportsmen believe there isn't enough cover in a drainage ditch to hide a rabbit, but it's not true. Many ditches and creek bottoms are loaded with brush, small tag alders and other low-growing trees and bushes, and a dandy buck can make himself right at home in these locations and never have to worry about most hunters."

Deer often use drainage ditches or creek bottoms as solid cover to move from one area to another, and this is doubly true during the rut. Such areas also offer protection from the wind, and good avenues of travel where animals can remain out of sight.

Two-Bit Swales

There's a type of fringeland cover I call a two-bit swale. Many are seemingly no bigger around than a quarter, but yet I've seen them produce some dandy whitetails.

Picture this: An open field ... I mean, a wide-open field with only a tiny alder or sumac-dotted swale for cover for hundreds of yards in any direction. The brushy postage-stamp-sized swale stands out in the field like a wart on a nose. My introduction to this type of fringeland deer habitat came while hunting rooster pheasants. We combed the field with my German Shorthair, and never turned a feather.

"Let's try that little swale," I said.

We didn't have anything to lose because my car was over the next hill past the swale. My buddy took one side, I took the other, and Fritz, my pointer, took the middle. I could see my friend, he could see me and we could both see the dog.

Fritz acted strange, not birdy, you know, but as if he were pointing a turtle or snake. He had that strange look bird dogs get when they know they are doing something wrong, like following a rabbit.

We looked but didn't see a thing until a whitetail buck burst out of the swale within 6 feet of us. The buck had been hiding, and we almost stepped on him. Even though we were searching the ground for birds ahead of the dog, we couldn't see the deer. He startled the hell out of us.

It pays to hunt tiny pockets of cover. Small swales are a good bet, and never should be overlooked. Hunt them the same way you'd hunt larger cover, and be ever mindful of your approach and the prevailing wind direction.

One thing about two-bit swales: they produce only on occasion, but more than one trophy buck has been taken from such fringeland areas. They are common wherever fringeland is found, and it really doesn't take much more cover to hide a deer than a rabbit or rooster pheasant.

A swale may be lower than the surrounding countryside or it may be higher. I've seen tiny knobs on top of a hill which were covered with brush, and have kicked deer from them as often as in low-lying swales. Treat each two-bit swale with respect because it just may produce the buck of a lifetime.

Swamps

When many deer hunters think of a swamp they see a sprawling area of cedar with more of it under water than above. There are these types of cedar swamps scattered across the northern tier of states from Minnesota east to the Atlantic Ocean, but such miles-square areas are not the ones fringeland deer hunters should be concerned with.

Fringeland, that area close to rural and suburban towns and farms, often may have a tiny tag alder or cedar swamp tucked back in a low corner where no one goes. It's these swamps, or some of the larger cattail swamps which are found along the Great Lakes, or pin oak swamps in the South, which can produce good numbers of whitetails.

A swamp is a relative thing. It can be an acre, 10 acres or several square miles of low ground. It is dense, hard to walk through and it holds deer. Cedar, spruce, balsam and tamarack are four types of trees commonly found in a swamp, and tag alders may ring the area.

There is a swamp not far from where I live, and as cedar swamps go it's a small one. But, it's a wet and wild tangle inside and deer hunters avoid the area like the plague because they hear persistent rumors of it containing quicksand and rattlesnakes.

I know the rumors, and they aren't true simply because my friends and I have been responsible for spreading the falsehoods. We are only trying to protect one small portion of mini-wilderness in a sea of fringeland cover. The swamp offers good deer hunting, and it isn't overrun with sportsmen. We intend to keep it that way so our children will have good deer hunting close to home in the years to come.

We spread our rumors in various ways. One time we were sitting in a coffee shop before our afternoon hunt. A coffee-drinking customer sitting nearby was togged out in camouflage clothing, and once he saw our similar clothing he posed the questions: "Are you from around here? Do you bowhunt?"

We nodded that we were and we did, and he continued, "What can you tell me about that little swamp three miles north of town?" That was our prime hunting spot, and my pardner didn't need any prodding to launch into his save-the-swamp spiel.

Lee rubbed his scruffy beard, and with a serious face stated, "That swamp is one bad spot. I tried hunting it four years ago, and although I get around well in the woods I didn't think I'd ever get out of there. There are bogs of boot-sucking mud, and I hear tell there are patches of quicksand scattered about. It's one mind-boggling spot, and very tough to hunt.

"I was lost almost from the moment I entered the swamp, and after wandering

This buck popped out of a two-bit swale and dashed off across marsh grass, in front of the hunter.

around for five hours trying to get my bearings I sat down under a cedar tree. I dozed off, and then woke up with the feeling something was looking at me. I looked around, but the feeling was too strong to shake. Something was watching me.

"Then, only five feet from my boots I spotted a Massasauga rattler staring at me from a coiled position. I was scared, and didn't know what to do but when I moved I know I set a new record for a sitting broad jump. I spent the night in that hellhole, and it wasn't until the next day the county sheriff and his posse spotted smoke from my campfire and led me out to safety.

"Yep, I know that swamp well, and I'll never go back into it," Lee concluded.

The young coffee drinker's eyes were as big as saucers by the time Lee ended his fabricated tale. The baldfaced lie touched all the bases; boot-sucking mud, quicksand, rattlesnakes, spending all night in an eerie swamp, a smoking campfire and the final irony of having a sheriff and posse root him out the next day. The sport didn't want any part of that tiny swamp so we sent him packing to another spot where deer existed and where he wouldn't get in our way.

Swamps hold deer for the simple reason few hunters really try to determine where the animals bed down or hide once hunting season begins. Such areas are made to order for the hunter with hipboots or chest-high waders, and the stamina to wade through mud, muck and water to reach a good hunting area.

It's not common knowledge, but under pressure a whitetail deer will stand for hours in chest-deep water. I once shot a little spikehorn which had been wounded by another hunter.

Firearms season had been open for several days, and Roger Kerby and Lee Blahnik were driving a thin strip of cedar swamp toward me. I heard a shot, another shot and a lot of yelling and screaming.

"He's in the water, and he's wounded," Kerby shouted. The nearby lake was covered with skim ice, but I could see where the buck had crashed through the ice almost to my stand. Try as I might I couldn't see the little buck although I could see blood on the ice. I searched the shoreline, and then saw what appeared to be a nose sticking up from the water. I scoped the area, and could barely see the deer's outline under the lake's surface.

I pulled up my thigh-high boots, and waded out toward the deer thinking it was dead. That buck spooked from the water, and I quickly brought the sights of my Ruger .44 Magnum down behind the shoulders and shot as he hit dry ground.

Paul Mickey once told me it's not uncommon to see deer standing in the water of a cattail or cedar swamp for hours. "I think whitetails believe it reduces their outline, and few are the hutners who will wade through water to hunt deer," he said.

Such areas are tough to hunt, and many sportsmen who bowhunt or gun a swamp are content to hunt the outside edges as whitetails come out to feed. Few are willing to chance becoming lost in a swamp tangle just for a deer, and that suits me just fine.

Hunters should look for good entrance and exit trails near a swamp, and ascertain whether the area is being used by does and fawns or by bucks. During hunting season a buck may enter and leave a swamp by routes different from those used by does and fawns, and these trails often follow other thick cover which intersects with swamp cover. Look for small seldom-used trails, and set up shop nearby.

Swamp terrain will hold deer only as long as good agricultural or wild foods are found nearby. A swamp will generally serve as a hideout or yarding area during winter months, but it's an area that is seldom productive unless hunting pressure is heavy.

There are other minor types of fringeland cover which hold deer, and they will be mentioned later in following chapters which discuss hunting techniques. Just remember, terrain and available food are two of the biggest reasons why whitetail deer will be found in a certain area. The only other thing which will pull whitetails into another location is the rut, and here we go.

CHAPTER 3

Deer During the Rut

The wide-antlered buck was tiptoeing along like he was walking on egg shells. One second his nose was in the air with his upper lip curled back as he sniffed something he liked, and the next second his nose was near the ground as he trailed a receptive doe. It was the rut—that period when sexually mature whitetail bucks think more with their hindquarters than with their head.

That was the scene when Roger Kerby arrived at one of his treestands. He guides deer hunters during the firearms season, but this was bow season. Kerby entered his treestand with little time to spare. The buck, although 150 yards away, was closing the gap as Kerby scaled the tree like a squirrel, readied an arrow on his Bear compound bow and dropped his camouflage face mask to cover glistening skin.

The buck was head-down and still coming, and it paid scant notice to the camo-clad hunter high in the sugar maple tree. The buck moved past Kerby at a steady pace, and it was grunting every step of the way. "I heard that buck coming for 100 yards," Kerby later said. "He was grunting like an oinker with every step, and just over the crest of the hill stood the waiting doe.

"It was a tense situation. If the doe saw any movement the game would be over for me."

His stand was near the junction of three well-used deer trails, and the buck was heading for the intersection like an 18-wheeler rolling for a truck stop, hot coffee and a pretty waitress. The massive buck passed within 10 yards of Kerby's treestand, and as the deer continued on his way the hunter came to full draw. He hesitated a moment, and sent the arrow deep into the animal's chest.

"The buck kicked like a rodeo bronc," Kerby said, "but I got full penetration and watched him run over the hill, still in hot pursuit of the doe. Fifty yards away he sagged to his knees, and fell for good."

Kerby's nine-point buck was massive, and it scored nearly 140 points in the complicated Pope & Young scorings. The score was more than enough to make the coveted record books. This fine trophy whitetail was taken during the rut.

The rut is one of the most misunderstood facets of whitetail deer hunting. The woods and bars, or wherever deer hunters gather, are rife with tales of wild-eyed bucks jumping from doe to doe like musical chairs. Some tales of swollen-necked bucks are true, but many are Ol' Hunter Tales which fall in the same category as Old Wive's Tales, fictional accounts of the Tooth Fairy and the Easter Bunny.

Modern whitetail deer research has taken place throughout North America in the last fifteen to twenty years, and the results of telemetry studies in several states and actual observation under controlled circumstances have shot holes in many theories concerning the rut.

What is the rut, when does it occur, what triggers it and what does it mean to fringeland deer hunters? These are questions that now can be answered. There are continuing studies being made of whitetail bucks and does, mating habits, rutting characteristics and the like, and it may be many years before biologists and scientists fully understand the rut. But for now the following information is based on scientific information and my personal observations of rutting whitetails over a period of nearly thirty years.

There may be some who will be willing to poke holes in my logic, but suffice it to say that I'm in the woods about eighty-five days during our ninety-day Michigan deer season, and I spend a good bit of time in September and January scouting prospective hunting locations for next season.

Whitetail deer become sexually active in the autumn of their second year, or when they are about 1½ years of age. Few bucks, however, will breed does at this time unless the bulk of the whitetail population in any given fringeland area are of the same age group. It's a sad but true fact that in many states or provinces where whitetail deer are common most bucks (and does) taken by hunters will be 1½ years of age, and few reach the ripe old age of five to seven years where antler growth is at its peak. Deer management is for numbers, not trophies, in many locations.

Doe breeding usually is done by dominant bucks, and these animals average 2½ to 3½ years old, but even 5½- or 6½-year-old deer will breed does. Young bucks (now you know where the term came from) are horny devils, and will try to breed receptive does, but more mature male deer will drive the youngsters off and do the breeding themselves.

Whitetail does become sexually mature going into the second year (at about 1½ years of age) although a few early-born fawns of less than one year may be bred late in the season.

It was once thought the rut was triggered by cold air, but if this were true many bucks in Alabama, Florida, Georgia, Louisiana and Texas would be frustrated and few southern does would be bred. Actually, cold weather is not what determines the onset of whitetail rutting.

The rut is triggered by a post-autumnal equinox phenomenon. As autumn days grow

Roger Kerby comes to full draw in his treestand. The stand was near the junction of three well-used deer trails, and Kerby knew a buck would come into range.

short, and daylight hours diminish, a whitetail will undergo a behavioral change which marks the onset of the rut. The time of the rut's onset varies from mid to late October in states like Michigan, Minnesota and Wisconsin to January in the deep South.

The decreasing hours of daylight results in a change in the function of the pituitary gland. Less sunlight makes the gland, whose primary purpose is to regulate body growth, function abnormally. The gland increases its secretion of testosterone (a male sex hormone) in bucks and progesterone (a female sex hormone) in doe deer. The increased levels of testosterone in a buck can cause him to react in different ways.

The oldest bucks in the area are the ones which eventually will do the actual breeding, although some breeding will be accomplished by lesser animals if few or no trophy animals are present in an area. The biggest bucks are the top honchos in the local herd's pecking order. Next in line are medium-aged antlered bucks, and the little spikehorns and forkhorns are down on the bottom rung of the ladder.

Once testosterone begins building in a buck the antler velvet dries, hardens and

Once velvet falls off its antlers a buck is ready to breed. This occurs when testosterone begins building in the animal. Then it stands scraping and rubbing ground and tree trunks.

begins falling off. The bucks paw at it with their feet or rub their antlers against bushes or small saplings and trees. These are functional movements used to remove antler velvet, and the deer are not making boundaries or leaving signs.

Deer, like humans, mature at different rates, and this single factor can help fringeland deer hunters account for good bucks early or late in the season. Although a whitetail buck can breed whenever his antlers are hard, nature has set up a schedule for does. Not all does come in heat at the same time, and this insures that the majority of the animals will be bred sometime during the rut.

The earliest does to come in heat generally are the oldest deer in the herd. They come in season early in the rut and well before younger does, and are in and out in about twenty-four hours. A buck must be quick on the trigger to sire offspring with these animals.

But (and here we're treading on somewhat controversial ground), these early does are the ones that will firmly establish which ground scrape will be the primary scrape used by bucks and does once the rut slides into full swing. The doe (usually an older animal) picks the spot, and it remains the primary dating grounds until the rut ends.

Rubs and Scrapes

A buck rub, during the rut, is a highway marker or billboard for other deer which states: "Hey gang, this is my turf and if you're smaller than I am look elsewhere for a date."

Buck rubs are a means by which male whitetails identify their boundaries (within reason) and notify other bucks they are in the area. They can signal their size and where they stand in the local hierarchy. All they tell a hunter is that the animal has been through the area. Bucks seldom return to rub on the same tree.

Rubs on small saplings or trees an inch or so in diameter generally are made by small bucks like spikehorns or small forkhorns. A rubbed tree of 2½ inches in diameter generally indicates the rub was made by a slightly older, larger deer, and these often are the 6s, 8s and occasional 10-point bucks.

John Weiss, an Ohio outdoor writer and deer hunter of note, once told me: "Look for rubs on the largest diameter trees in the area; especially those from 3 to 5 inches in diameter on cedars, pines or smooth-barked saplings. These were made by the largest deer with the heaviest antlers in the area."

I agree, and have seen a few buck rubs on 6- to 8-inch trees in one of my hunting areas. I saw that buck, and didn't get him, but he was a candidate for the Boone & Crockett Club and would have placed high in the standings.

Fringeland deer hunters must look for savaged trees or saplings once the rut begins. Some deer in anger or frustration will destroy a tree while making a rub, and this is one important clue to look for when conducting a search for available food and proper terrain.

Ground scrapes appear like magic. This one is small, and indicates a young buck.

George Nichols examines a typical scrape. It measures about 2 by 3 feet.

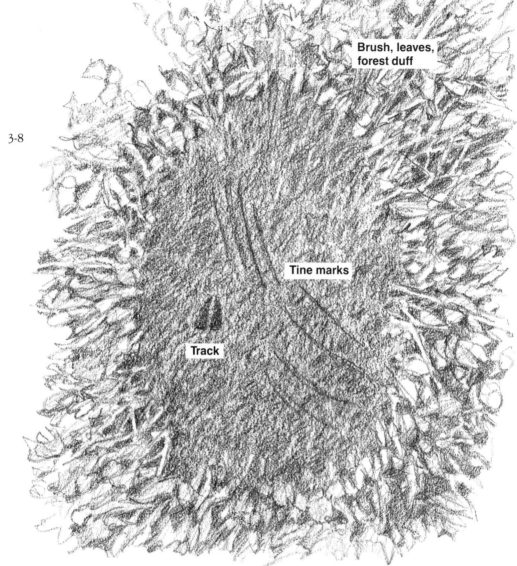

3-8

Brush, leaves, forest duff

Tine marks

Track

A scrape is generally oval or egg shaped. It is free of brush, leaves and forest duff, and usually has a deer track within the perimeter.

Many scrapes smell of urine. Lee Blahnik checks the freshness of this one.

Ground scrapes, or mating scrapes as they are often called, are another clue to the rut being underway. Just remember, however, that ground scrapes appear like magic—like mushrooms after a spring rain—sometime from late September through December depending on latitude. There are some writers, and many deer hunters, who figure each scrape is a primary scrape and discount secondary or boundary scrapes as being made "by little guys." Probably more misinformation has been spread about scrapes than any other facet of deer hunting.

Scrapes vary in size, from a small pawed-apart area to something the size of a large dinner table. Small scrapes generally mean small bucks, and larger scrapes usually are made by the big boys.

The average whitetail scrape will measure 2 by 3 or 4 feet, and is oval or egg-shaped. I've seen an active, primary scrape 5 by 10 feet made by a huge old buck that no one ever shot. He probably died of old age during a hard winter, but it wasn't until after he'd spread his seed through the local doe population.

It pays to remember that primary scrapes are picked by the oldest does in the area, and it's often done during the first brief rutting period of the season. In my area this occurs in early October; seldom will the rut begin peaking until October 20 to 25 when the majority of whitetail does begin coming in season. The old gals set the stage for what will happen later in the month.

A whitetail scrape means little by itself. It can mean several bucks are using the area and staking out their terrain, or it can mean several lesser-antlered and immature bucks have been through the area. More than one buck and more than one doe will visit any one primary scrape. If small bucks approach, swiftly drift in and out after whizzling it down with urine, then it probably means a larger, more dominant buck is coming regularly to the site or is nearby. Nearby sign or spoor in the scrape can indicate whether the scrape belongs to the main man or one of lesser importance.

A few hunters of my acquaintance go out with spotting scopes or binoculars long before deer season opens, and knowing that whitetails invariably scrape in the same locations year after year, study scraping sites from afar. They want to know in advance which patch of pawed ground will attract the big, old doe.

One woodlot I hunt is bordered by a long fallow field. The woods to the north are never scraped while the edge of the woodlot on the south side will have a minimum of a dozen scrapes along a 150-yard border. Only one of these twelve or so scrapes will be the primary scrape, and it's here that several big bucks have been shot over the years.

In scrapes made by big, sexually mature bucks which are ready to breed, the ground will appear to have been worked over thoroughly. The buck will paw all forest duff away down to the bare ground, and often one or two hoof prints will show in the moistened earth. Look for antler tine marks and determine just how far apart they are. If they measure from 4 to 6 inches or more apart, there's at least one trophy buck in the neighborhood.

About 85 percent of all scrapes are located under overhanging limbs which are 3 to 5 feet off the ground. Overhanging limbs often are chewed or appear to have been nib-

This doe isn't ready to breed. Her tail is clamped tight although she left a fresh scrape.

bled by deer. Actually, what happens is a buck will hold the end of the branch in his mouth, and rub the branch across his preorbital gland at the corner of the eye to deposit a secretion. If there are no overhanging branches near a scrape then check nearby bushes because often a buck will ravage low-growing shrubs and rub secretions from the gland across the bush to indicate his presence.

The direction a buck travels can be determined from the scrape. This knowledge can work for the hunter provided he knows how to read what the scrape sign is telling him.

A buck will paw the earth while freshening a scrape. Almost nine times out of ten, if the earth is pawed toward a bedding area that buck is visiting it in late afternoon or early evening as he leaves the bedding site. If the dirt is scraped away away from a bedding site and toward some distant spot where deer are suspected to be feeding, chances are equally as good the animal checks his scrape in the morning on the way to bed down.

I've watched countless hunters check scrapes for freshness, and then kick leaves or dirt on top of the scrape. "Just trying to see if the buck is checking the scrape," they say.

Seldom do they realize human odor is associated with such acts. If the hunter is wearing a leather boot, it will transmit a human odor to the leaves and dirt. Many hunters wear all-rubber boots and never cover a fresh scrape.

A buck does many things when he visits a primary scrape whether it is early (during the false rut), during the main rut or in December when unbred or young does are serviced. (This latter rutting period normally takes place twenty-eight to thirty days after the main rut occurs and is Nature's way of seeing that all breedable does are bred. In my area this last rut will take place in early to mid-December, and actually represents one of the best times to take a trophy whitetail buck. Bucks will paw the earth, rake it with antler tines and urinate down their back legs and into the scrape. Some young bucks who are frustrated by a lack of female companionship may masturbate and ejaculate into the scrape. All this is accompanied by a chewing of overhead branches, rubbing of said branches across the preorbital gland and a general panting and/or grunting.

What isn't commonly known is the part played by the doe during this rutting process. Go back a few pages and reread the part about an old doe picking the site of the primary scrape. She knows where it is, as does every buck and younger doe within a mile.

A doe ready to be bred will advance on the scrape and leave her calling card by urinating down her back legs and defecating. The urine carries traces of her estrus, and advertises that she is in heat and is ready—really ready—to be serviced by a buck. The doe either waits for the buck or goes to him.

A buck may be an antsy fellow and willing to take a ride on any doe in season, but he knows where that primary scrape is located and is never too far from the action. The doe will signal her intent in the scrape, and may actually hang around the scrape for many long minutes waiting for the buck to appear. If he doesn't, she tracks him down

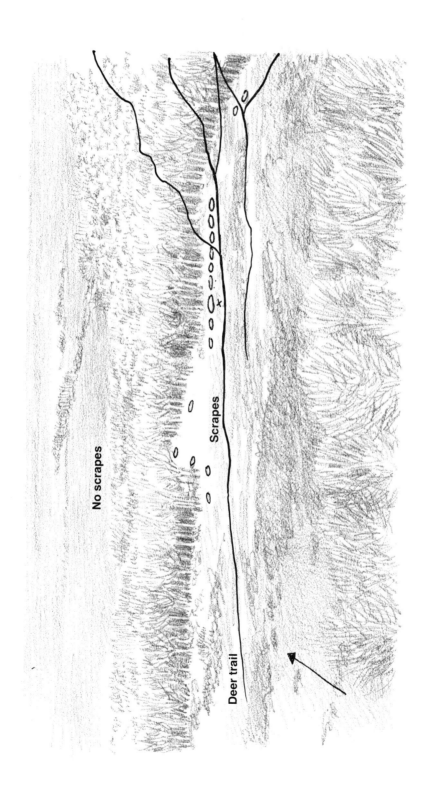

No scrapes

Scrapes

Deer trail

Feeding areas

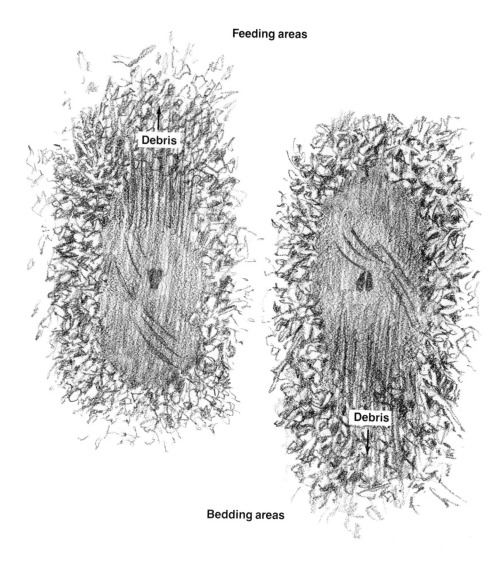

Debris

Debris

Bedding areas

Observe the direction of dirt and duff thrown by a buck checking a scrape. It can tell you what time of day he usually visits the spot. Debris thrown toward bedding area means buck scrapes in evening or late afternoon on way to feed. Debris thrown toward feeding area means buck scrapes in early morning on way to feeding area.

Opposite: A woodlot I hunt borders on a fallow field. There usually are a dozen or more scrapes along one edge, none along the other.

39

from scent secreted between his hooves. She's looking for action, and may wait for hours within 200 yards of a primary scrape hoping he shows up. If he doesn't, she goes looking for him.

Suppose a hunter kills the buck and leaves the poor doe wondering what happened? She merely trots off and finds another buck who is willing to stand for her.

Scrapes, during the rut, are a thing to marvel at because they are like billboards advertising who is doing what to whom. The hunter should watch for bucks that visit a scrape and find a doe's calling card. And bucks do visit scrapes. In areas densely populated with deer a buck may visit a scrape three or four times daily. The reverse is true where fringeland whitetails are few and far between—the buck may spend two or three days visiting other scrapes he's discovered in his travels. A doe remains in estrus about one day (some twenty-three to twenty-eight hours), and goes out if she's not bred.

High rubber boots worn by George Nichols will prevent his leaving telltale scent behind. Nichols would not ordinarily kneel on the ground, but did so to point out this scrape near a cornfield.

A ready-to-breed buck rubs his preorbital gland across a sapling, leaving a scent for other deer.

These unbred deer are the ones that will come into heat later in the year. It's been documented that in areas where deer numbers are high a single big buck may impregnate some thirty does during the rut.

Bucks may check their scrapes during the morning, afternoon, evening or after dark when the rut is peaking, but they do so with caution, and here's where a deer hunter can learn something. I've seen bow and gun hunters sitting within ten yards of a primary scrape, and they never see a buck. That's because bucks often check a scrape from downwind. If a sweet-looking doe is ready and waiting a buck will scent her from downwind. He'll also know if a hunter is there.

Bearing in mind that many bucks circle downwind to check a scrape, the hunter

This little spikehorn came to a scrape shortly after it had been visited by a doe, and the young hunter popped him. He wasn't hunting trophies, and a spikehorn was just dandy.

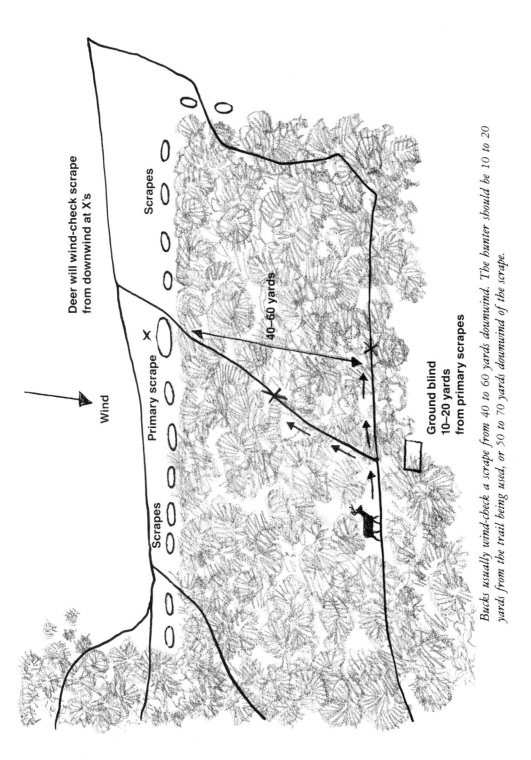

Deer will wind-check scrape from downwind at X's

Scrapes

40–60 yards

Primary scrape

Wind

Scrapes

Ground blind
10–20 yards
from primary scrapes

Bucks usually wind-check a scrape from 40 to 60 yards downwind. The hunter should be 10 to 20 yards from the trail being used, or 50 to 70 yards downwind of the scrape.

This cornfed buck was shot at a scrape bordering the cornfield. It checked the scrape at noon, and this farmer has venison for winter.

should avoid sitting in a ground blind or treestand near open terrain. Learn to anticipate where the buck will appear, and how he will wind-check the scrape area from
downwind. Learn to locate the nearest heavy cover in which to conceal yourself, and
resist the temptation to sit near open areas where you can see a country mile. Bucks
hate such areas, and frequent them only after dark.

Leave enough open areas through which to shoot, but position yourself downwind
from where you suspect the buck will show himself. A big buck often will wind-check
a scrape from as far as 50 yards downwind; your hunting position should be at least 60
yards from the scrape you are watching.

Some hunters believe that bucks visit these scrapes only during morning and evening. "Look for 'em at daybreak or dusk," the pundits say.

Believe it if you will, but note that several friends and I have shot bucks at scrapes
with bow or firearm at all hours of the day. I've never seen a bulletin board which states
that bucks will arrive at such and such a time and leave at another specific time. I do
know I've shot bucks visiting scrapes at high noon, and I've shot them in the evening.
I have launched an arrow or two at rutting bucks at dawn, but I've never scored in the
morning.

Deer of any age during the rut are more active than at any other time of the year. It
makes little difference to them whether they feel the urge at high noon, or three in the
afternoon. If the doe is ready, and the buck is looking for action it won't make any
difference how old the animals are providing they are old enough to breed.

One thing hunters must keep in mind is that food and terrain play an important part
in a deer's everyday activities. A doe has to eat to keep her strength during pregnancy,
but a buck does not. Some bucks feed between bouts in the willows, but many do not
and enter the winter losing up to 30 percent of their body weight. If the winter season
is rough, many perish because they have lost so much body weight during the rut.
Does seldom have this problem although they can and will lose weight after concep-
tion and during winter months. Some hunters who learn where deer (especially the
does) feed, take up stands nearby to intercept willing bucks. By the same token, many
bucks have learned that feeding sites are excellent places to find does ready to be bred.

Bucks often bed down within 200 yards of a primary scrape, and get up to wind-
check the area as often as once each hour during the day. They may stand close to the
scrape after dark, or go rustling around a feeding site in hopes of finding a receptive
doe.

Hunting Tactics

We know about rutting deer. But how do we hunt specific types of fringeland terrain during or near the rut? The rut in my state occurs during the early bow season but
is winding down by the time the mid-November firearms season begins. But it is differ-

ent in each state. Some states prohibit deer hunting during the rut. God only knows for what reason although state biologists often say it is to protect the deer.

The peak of the whitetail rut changes according to latitude and somewhat according to longitude. The farther north one goes the earlier the rut begins and ends. The farther south hunters travel for their sport the later the rut will be. Determine rutting dates in each area to be hunted, and plan your trip accordingly.

One of the best ways (I've experimented with them for years, and exclusively for the last three years) to take rutting bucks is with deer scents. I shoot my two bucks each year using the stuff and occasionally a buck in another state.

If you were to walk into any bar or sporting goods store in whitetail counry it may be possible to find someone willing to fight in defense of cover (masking) or sex scents while deer hunting. On the other hand, should you speak too loudly denouncing the effectiveness of such scents the barroom bully who uses them may take exception and do a remodeling job on your face.

The question is: Do they work, and if so why? The answer may fall between the cracks for many sportsmen, but in reality scents work for some and not for other hunters. I know they work for me, and the last buck I shot with a bow is a good example.

A good sex scent is Tink's #69 Doe-In-Rut Buck Lure.

He stood for long minutes with his nose buried in a 35mm film canister filled with Tink's #69 Doe-In-Rut Buck Lure. Coincidence? Hardly, because it was the sixth such buck I've shot in three years under similar circumstances.

Deer are extremely conscious of human odor during the rut. A whisper of human odor drifting down to a sex-crazed buck will not act as a love potion on him but will probably have about the same effect as a cold shower. I prefer using skunk or fox masking scent, and generally avoid coyote scent because these animals are predators on young deer. Fox or skunk scent is a common odor in most fringeland areas, and deer have been known to investigate these odors.

Whenever possible I position myself downwind in heavy cover from where I suspect rutting bucks will come. I then position three canisters of skunk scent downwind of my stand, and position doe urine or a Doe-in-Rut lure where I expect the buck to appear. I want to position the animal for a good shot, and many times will locate my stand and doe scent slightly to the left of my position so I'll have a shot at the animal as it goes away from me. This allows me to come to full draw with my bow or raise my rifle while the buck's back is to me.

Some hunters create false scrapes, and this can be productive if they are cognizant of the wind direction at all times. They create a scrape where they wish it to be, and then soak a rag in doe scent and drag it past their stand. Theoretically, the buck will catch the scent, follow it to the scrape, suspect the old girl has split and go looking for her along the drag line. Do this in thick cover near a scrape.

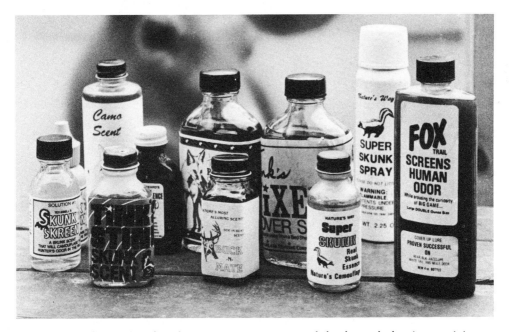

Several different types of masking or cover scents. Fox and skunk are the best in my opinion.

Some hunters prefer to have a sex scent on their clothing even when they sit in a treestand. I've seen some strange things in my time, but I've yet to see a whitetail doe up a tree, and I suspect any buck close enough to smell doe urine or doe-in-rut odors in a tree would think he'd flipped out. That is, if the hunter didn't shoot him.

Foreign odors such as gasoline, oil or cooking smells are to be avoided during any deer hunting period. They are not natural odors, and a sportsman would be far better off storing his hunting clothing in a plastic bag filled with cedar or pine boughs. Fringeland deer are accustomed to smelling cedar, pine or even oak leaves, and the odor does not signify danger to them. Human scent on clothing and/or boots will hang in the air or on the ground for hours under certain atmospheric conditions, and will ruin your chance for a shot.

If necessary take the long way around to reach your hunting area, even during the rut, and wear high rubber boots. Sneak into the area as quietly as possible, and try to be there thirty minutes to an hour before you expect deer to start moving. Avoid walking through the location you plan to hunt, and be ever mindful of a deer's nose and its ability to sniff out danger.

Ground blind or treestand for rutting bucks? It's a toss-up for many people, and this topic will be covered in a later chapter. I'd just like to add that whichever way you choose to hunt—on the ground or in a tree—make sure some cover is behind you to break up your silhouette. Given the choice I'd rather sit in the open with cover behind me than sit in the open with something in front. Frontal cover hampers hunter vision, and reduces the chances for a shot.

CHAPTER 4

Ground Blinds
or Treestands

Whenever and wherever two or more deer hunters gather across this continent you'll find an argument that rages like a brush fire ahead of a heat-charged wind. The argument—whether ground blinds are as effective as treestands.

"Treestands are best because any breeze will blow human scent over or away from approaching whitetails," a tree climber will tell you. "Besides, a tree hunter can see more of the area and watch deer movements. Also, deer seldom expect danger from above."

"Nuts," retorts a hidebound ground hunter. "No one can be comfortable up high while worrying about falling from a tree. You squirm around too much for personal safety, and it's difficult to make a good shot at a deer from 20 feet up."

The arguments are familiar because I've been on both sides of the fence. It's like a writer arguing with an editor, and vice versa; misconceptions on both sides keep the argument going.

I once was a confirmed ground blind hunter. It made little difference whether I was bow or gun hunting; I didn't want any part of a tree. Trees, like horses, were two things I hadn't learned to trust. Tree limbs break at inopportune times, or winter-chilled fingers release at the wrong moment, and I'd crashed down through branches on more than one occasion. I always liked both feet on the ground.

It was Claude Pollington who lifted me off the ground and into one of his treestands. He begged and pleaded with me for a month to try a tree, and I finally relented . . . against my better judgment.

"Dave, there's a nice eight-pointer coming in almost every night to work that scrape at Matt's set," Pollington cajoled. "It's a low stand, and even if you fall it is only 10 feet. You'll shoot a buck tonight if you can overcome your squeamishness about being in a tree."

He'd been working on me for a year, and often I would almost give in before remembering tree stands from other years. Bruises fade with time, but the sickening feeling in the pit of your stomach as you bounce downward from limb to limb was something I no longer needed.

"C'mon," he begged. "Just be careful, don't slip and sit still. The buck will be within 20 feet of you, and it's a dog shot."

"OK," I whined. I would try, but I wasn't one bit happy about it.

Now, mind you, I was not afraid of height; it's just that I was petrified of falling. Over the years I've broken my back twice while bopping around the outdoors, and the thought of doing it again from a tree was not appealing.

It was an easy climb into the pine tree. The branches were evenly spaced, and a Baker treestand was firmly anchored to the tree. Heavy pine boughs stood out behind the stand to break my outline, and a well-used scrape was 20 feet down and to my left. It was made to order for a right-handed bowhunter.

When I'd climbed into position, sat down and readied my equipment, I relaxed. The bow handle hung from a nail within inches of my left hand, and the Game Tracker string was knotted firmly behind a Bear broadhead. I flipped the camo mask down over my face, leaned back against the tree trunk and waited.

"Hey, this isn't too bad," I thought. "The visibility is good, and the breeze is blowing my scent away from the scrape. If a rutting buck tries to circle to wind-check the scrape, and crosses the open area, he'll have to pass within range."

An hour passed, and whitetail bucks were sparring 200 yards away in an open field. Does stood around like bored spectators at a bar fight, and I wondered if a buck would show below me.

Dusk was rapidly settling over the countryside when I heard the sound of soft footsteps behind the treestand. The sound stopped. Then two minutes later I heard another step.

I didn't dare risk swiveling around for a look. Claude had cautioned me to sit still and wait for the buck to step into the open after he was satisfied the coast was clear. A minute later the buck took another step, paused and stepped almost into the open.

I could see his nose, the eight-point rack and 3 inches of neck, but he needed to take two or three more steps before I could come to full draw. The buck swiveled his head and stared over his rump in the direction from which he had come. I used that moment to silently lift my bow off the nail.

My fingertips wrapped around the bowstring, one above and two below the nocking point. My eyes were riveted to the buck, and I moved only when his attention strayed from my tree. Each movement I made was a study in slowness; an inch at a time my left arm straightened out and lifted the bow into position to make my draw.

The buck stood as motionless as a granite statue. His nostrils quivered, and his eyes seemed to bore holes through everything in sight. This jasper was wary and in no rush to make a dumb move.

His neck was swollen and appeared grotesque from the rutting activity. Inch by inch his rounded neck stretched forward like a snake to sniff the scrape, but he still had to move 4 feet to give me a clear shot at the heart-lungs area behind his front shoulder.

He apparently liked what his sniffer told him. A piglike grunt rumbled up from his chest, and he took two steps forward into the scrape. His feet were a blur as he savaged the ground, and then he stopped as suddenly as he started. With a slight movement he turned his head away and began rubbing his preorbital gland across a nearby bush. He was in full rutting frenzy, and now was oblivious to anything else.

I came to a full draw, locked the junction of my thumb and forefinger behind my jaw bone, mentally inserted the tip of my index finger in the corner of my mouth to make a rock-solid anchor point. I laid my 10-yard sight pin low behind the buck's front shoulder. The release was smooth, and the arrow pegged the deer through the engine room with an audible "thunk," like rapping on a ripe watermelon.

The eight-pointer smashed through the nearby tag alder swale, circled once and headed toward an open field 200 yards away. My Game Tracker stringer was peeling out as if a big chinook salmon was taking line.

Claude Pollington (right) helps me drag out a nice buck I shot from his son's favorite treestand.

This luxurious treestand was built by rock star Ted Nugent. It has sliding panels that conceal the hunter until he can shoot.

"Fish on!" I hollered, holding my bow aloft, because that's just what it feels like when an arrow-shot deer runs off trailing string. I was elated because my jittery feeling over being in a treestand had paid off with a shot at a rutting buck at spitting distance.

Seconds later the string stuttered, stopped, inched forward a few more feet and stopped for good. The deer was down, and all indications pointed to a dead buck.

I followed the string and gathered it up along the heavy blood trail. The eight-point buck with the swollen neck had traveled 75 yards with a neatly severed heart, and had died on the run.

Pollington was as excited as I was. "See," he joked, "treestands aren't so bad after all. You've been missing a bet for years."

I had to admit there is a time and place for treestands. But I'm also convinced ground blinds serve a useful purpose and wouldn't want anyone to think the foregoing anecdote is an all-out endorsement of treestands. The trick of taking fringeland deer with something approaching regularity is to know when and where to choose a ground blind over a treestand and when an elevated position would increase the chance of success. In some areas whitetail deer have been hunted so much from treestands they are spooky and will walk along with nose in the air trying to see hunter movement in nearby trees.

A familiarity with food sources and terrain features can help hunters make the decision to hunt at ground or treetop level. The hardnosed sportsman who cannot or will not switch from ground blinds to treestands, or back again as situations dictate, is stubborn and is lowering his odds of scoring on fringeland bucks.

Both ground blinds and treestands have something to offer bow or firearms hunters. We'll take a long look at both, and offer suggestions on when, where and how they can be used best in fringeland areas.

Ground Blinds

The buck moved as silently as a patch of drifting ground fog. He stopped every 5 feet and tested the air by raising his nose to the wind. Each pause lasted a minute before the buck would move again.

I'd been watching the buck from my ground blind in southeastern Tennessee as he eased from a soy bean field. He would stop, look up and around in all directions before heading for a finger of oak-filled woods along a brushy fencerow.

My ground-level surveillance was in order because this eight-pointer apparently had been hunted from treestands for so long he had forgotten his basic training. As he moseyed along he spent too much time looking up into trees and too little time scanning nearby ground areas.

The buck was neatly screened by thick brush along the fencerow, and was hard to see, but each step he took brought him closer to my hay-bale blind at the edge of a small woodlot. He was heading my way, and my hands perspired as they gripped the stock of my Remington .270.

The deer seemed overly curious about a weathered oak along the fencerow, and several times would stop to stare up into the branches. Then it became obvious; the buck was looking at an old treestand instead of ahead and to either side along the ground.

The buck finally satisfied himself the treestand was empty, and made his move like a race horse leaving the starting gate. He shot out into the open field within 25 yards of my ground blind, stopped and turned back for a final look at the treestand.

I raised the .270, slid the crosshairs and post down low behind his front shoulder and caressed the trigger. The shot sounded as loud as a cannon in the fall air, and the buck sank to his knees and over on his side like a deflated balloon.

That Tennessee buck had tunnel vision. He had learned about the danger of treestands and hunters who bowhunt or gun from elevated platforms, but he had forgotten his basic training. He'd forgotten about dangers from ground level, and this happens in heavily hunted areas.

A Minnesota deer hunter I know, bowhunting near his home on a daily basis, has yet to claim a whitetail buck after six years of hunting from treestands. Yet he bagged a buck the second day out while bowhunting from a makeshift ground blind so ugly it looked as if a pack of hoboes had used it for summer camp.

"I can't understand it," he told me before I suggested a shift to a ground blind. "I see bucks almost every day, but the steep angles and intervening brush make it difficult to obtain a clean killing shot. Either I miss completely, a twig deflects my arrow or the buck seems aware of the presence and shies away out of range."

Claude Pollington feels treestand hunting is the best thing to happen to bowhunting since the advent of the Michigan two-deer season. But, he maintains elevated platforms are not for everyone.

"The angles are totally different when shooting down from treestands located 15 to 30 feet in the air," Pollington says. "A straight down shot is difficult for some bow-

Roger Kerby sits in a treestand and waits for a buck to come within shooting range. He's one of the best hunters I've ever known.

This buck is looking up, and the hunter is slightly off balance in his Baker treestand. The buck jumped the string, and he missed the shot. In heavily hunted areas bucks do look up.

hunters and too many fear heights. Some cannot shoot accurately from any height, and others wiggle so much with insecurity that a whitetail can spot the movement 100 yards away."

That's exactly what the Tennessee whitetail was looking for. The treestand he inspected for many minutes was 30 feet up the tree, and those who climbed up and sat in it must have suffered the willies.

Me, I used to break out in cold sweats whenever I climbed into a treestand. I was as nervous as a teenager on his first date with a pretty cheerleader, and would ruin any hope for a shot by constantly fidgeting around or checking to see if my safety belt was fastened.

It took that eight-pointer on Pollington's property to make me see that there really is no need to climb 25 or 30 feet up a tree to score on a fringeland whitetail. The lower heights are fine providing one knows the score and how to hunt from treestands.

Many hunters, including this writer, are convinced that in heavily hunted whitetail areas, where countless treestands hold bow or gun hunters, whitetails spend as much or more time looking up as they do scanning ground level sites for danger. All the old arguments about elevated stands concealing movement, circulating hunter scent far from the area and allowing for better shots are no longer valid. The old saw about whitetails never looking up has been disproved so many times it's a wonder anyone but the village idiot still believes it. Deer do look up, and as surely as does drop spring fawns, these newborn whitetails will learn to look up as well. It's in their genes.

There are ground blinds and there are others which to the uninitiated may pass for ground blinds. Some are abominable creations which look more like windowed outhouses than a place from which to hunt whitetails, and yet some are works of art although they aren't pretty. A ground blind need not be fancy, but it must be functional. To be functional the ground blind must blend in with its surroundings, offer a clear lane for a shot and serve to break up the outline of the hunter. Anything less is a waste of time.

My ground blinds may not be pretty, but they are functional and in tune with nature. I prefer simple cornstalk blinds when hunting in or near standing corn; a hay-bale blind in areas where hay is common. Pit blinds are possibly the best of all.

These blinds blend with their surroundings and are located at ground level where shoulder-height shots are the rule rather than the exception. A ground hunter does not have to turn himself into a corkscrew to let off a shot as a treestand hunter often must do. He only has to rise to one knee to shoot into the vital chest area of a deer.

For generations, hunters hunted whitetails from ground blinds. The bowman or gunner would pick a spot according to the prevailing wind direction and position himself in a natural hide downwind from where he expected the animal to appear. He chose wrong   e often than not because it's difficult to anticipate the actions of any animal.

From the day it hits the ground as a gangly, long-legged fawn to the day it dies, a whitetail is a high-strung animal. It is as explosive as a keg of dynamite with a sputter-

A functional ground blind being used by Kay Richey. She sat out slightly farther than is needed for this photo; in practice she'd be in the shadows.

Paul Kerby sits in a hay-bale blind waiting for deer. If he crouched farther back in the shadows, he would not be seen by approaching deer.

Herb Boldt uses a hay-bale blind to watch fringeland areas for whitetail deer. Deer are used to hay bales in most farming areas.

Sitting with his back against a tree, Herb Boldt waits for his buck downwind from an active deer trail.

58

Preseason scouting paid off for guide Roger Kerby (left) and Andy Simpkins.

ing fuse and spooks easily. I've seen does shy from a bird flying overhead, and I've watched bucks and does bolt at the sight of a squirrel running across a limb or across the ground. Every sense is alert for danger.

A good ground blind must be positioned properly. Preseason scouting is essential in order to locate the wild foods and agricultural crops fringeland deer feed on. The next step is to locate where deer bed down, where they feed and how they move to and from bedding or feeding areas. Further scouting will reveal those little used escape trails bucks often follow when danger threatens.

In each hunting area, note the prevailing wind direction, and watch deer to see how they travel under different wind conditions. Try to locate a ground hide downwind from where you expect deer to come from; this often varies from morning to evening. Claude Pollington's Buck Pole Deer Camp is an example because many truck crops consumed by deer on his land are located east of the prime bedding locations, and the prevailing winds are from the west in the evening and east in the morning. Whitetails on Pollington's spread must move east in the evening with the wind at their back to reach feeding areas, and move west in the morning with the wind again at their back to reach bedding locations. Certainly, some deer will move crosswind and some return to bedding areas early enough to avoid the prevailing wind switch, but nonetheless these animals move downwind on a daily basis.

Much of what I know about placement of ground blinds I learned at Pollington's deer camp. He chooses natural sites for ground blinds, and uses pit blinds whenever possible which place at least half of the hunter below ground level. Truck crops in his area include winter wheat, buckwheat, corn and alfalfa, and the blinds are located near bedding or feeding areas.

"One of the finest ground blinds in the world where hay is grown is several rectangular hay-bales placed downwind of an area where deer feed or near a trail leading into a feeding area," Pollington maintains. "Whitetails are accustomed to seeing hay-bales in this country, and the natural odor of the hay can help offset the human scent if an unexpected wind switch takes place. Position hay-bale bowhunter blinds 20 to 25 yards downwind from the trail, and about 50 yards away for rifle hunters."

Such hay-bale blinds are hotspots near feeding areas if they are left standing during a late-season bow season. Second-cutting hay is avidly eaten by whitetail deer. On one occasion I was trying to fill my doe tag in mid-December at Pollington's spread and had deer eating my blind with me inside it. They didn't get my scent because I was inside the hay, and I later shot a doe at 6 feet as she walked past the opening of my blind. That, my friends, is close shooting.

Pit blinds are a challenge to prepare, and even more of a challenge to hunt from. These dug-out pits can be placed along trails in wooded areas, near the edges of swales or swamps, in the middle or along the edges of open agricultural fields or wherever deer move. The trick is to locate them in the proper area, and to dig them in such a manner that bow or gun hunters can comfortably shoot. Too many pit blinds are far too small, and the hunter often is skylighted.

Natural sites, like this ground blind being used by Claude Pollington, are preferred by some hunters in fringeland country. Note fields, woods, and low swales behind Pollington. This site is called Execution Knob for a very good reason—it produces plenty of big bucks.

Dig a pit approximately 3 to 3½ feet deep, and at least 4 feet wide (from front to back) and 4 to 5 feet wide (from side to side). Dig the back of the pit down 24 to 30 inches, pack it down firmly and use it as a seat. The balance of the pit should be dug to the proper depth for feet and legs, and ample room is needed. Locate a pit blind downwind from the deer trail to be watched, but position it so brush, corn stalks or trees will break up your outline from behind.

One of the finest pit blinds I've hunted in was along a cornfield in North Carolina. A few stalks stood in front of my blind, and heavy webbings of corn stalks was woven together behind me. Corn grew on both sides, and deer moved through the cropland to feed each evening. One afternoon just before dusk a doe and two evenly matched bucks entered a nearby soybean field adjacent to the corn. I watched them from a distance of 60 yards . . . much too far for my bow. Then, another buck entered the soybeans, took

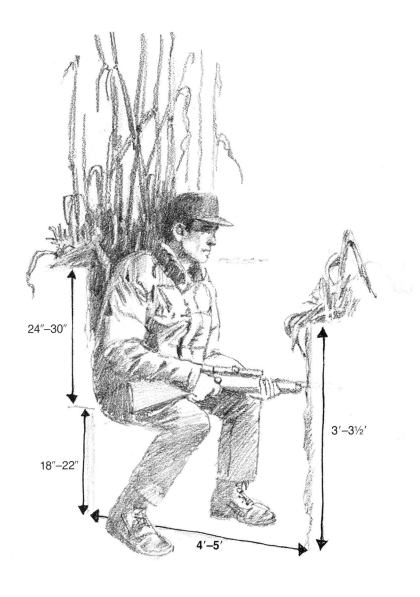

24"–30"

18"–22"

3'–3½'

4'–5'

The proper dimensions of a pit blind. The best ones are dug in front of corn stalks or tree limbs which break up the hunter's silhouette.

Opposite: Hay-bale blinds placed downwind of natural feeding areas are sure bets during the gun season. Kay Richey uses her binoculars to check the area; then she'll sit down to shoot with her .270.

63

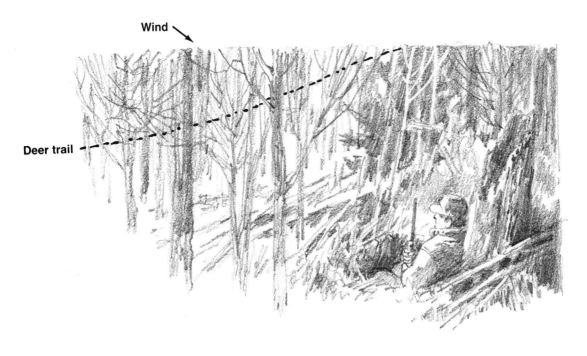

Wind

Deer trail

During gun season, dig pit blinds downwind from an active deer trail in thick, heavy cover.

one look at the other bucks and scattered them like a tornado scattering chickens.

The doe was not up to playing his rutting games, so she hied herself into the corn away from the big bully. He pranced around, looked tough and tried to con one of the little guys into a scrap. I wanted him, but I was trying to keep one eye on the doe who was feeding and moving down the corn toward me.

I kept one eye on the jumbo buck, and the other on the doe, and was getting cross-eyed trying to watch both animals. The buck stood his ground, but the doe kept feeding toward me at a steady pace. She was 20 yards away in the corn, and rapidly feeding my way.

The buck made a move to intercept her, and I slowly raised my camouflage-covered bow for a shot. I'd shoot if he approached within 25 yards before the doe reached my pit blind. Unfortunately, she fed right up to my blind, poked her nose through the corn stalks and got a full dose of human scent. She nearly blew my ears off with her snort, and then blew snot all over my face when she learned what was sharing her cornfield. The buck disappeared while I cleaned crud off my camo mask.

Pit blinds are deadly when properly positioned in heavy cover. Bucks, in particular, are cautious about entering open fields but often will move through heavy cover in a more casual manner. A trick a New York buddy of mine uses is to locate a good, well-used buck trail. Once he knows a buck is using that trail (he locates the trail in the early fall before hunting season begins) he determines the wind direction, digs a pit near a toppled tree or brush pile and then walks away from it for two months. He doesn't set foot in the pit again until opening day of the New York firearms season. He then circles around downwind, walks upwind to the pit and climbs in with everything he needs to spend the day. Most years he will slap a nice buck up alongside the neck with a "thutty-thutty," and the hunt is over before lunch.

His pit blind is always located in heavy cover, and along seldom-used trails. He feels that once opening-day guns start barking any bucks in the area will head for heavy cover. Those bucks in his area sneak along through the thick brush, and eventually one will pass within shooting range.

Stump blinds are common in parts of Canada, northern Wisconsin, northern Michigan and Minnesota and throughout Maine. Stumps, usually cedar stumps burned over years ago in a forest fire, make fantastic ground blinds if properly positioned. Locate stump blinds (stumps can be knocked apart, and repositioned in ideal spots) where a

Claude Pollington peers from a pit blind near heavy cover. Note that nothing shows except his face, hat and rifle. If he were not posing for a photo, a deer wouldn't see him until the shot went off.

gun hunter can watch a good area. One Ontario fringeland area I once hunted had been burned over years before, and blackened stumps dotted the edge of an alfalfa field. Deer fed in the field in early morning and again just before dark, and this stump blind blended in with the surrounding environment. It stood there for years, and the deer (and bear) didn't seem to mind. Each year my buddy shot his deer and a bear from the same stump blind.

One other thing before we move on to treestands: A hunter in a ground blind will usually get a closer shot at a whitetail than will a hunter in a treestand. I could recount any number of bucks and does which I shot from ground blinds at 10 yards or less. The same holds true for whitetail deer traveling through those areas we define as fringeland. Much of this country is a mix of open and brushy or woods-filled land, and visibility is good. A human that moves in a treestand 100 yards away must look like a kingsize woodpecker to an approaching whitetail deer.

Treestands

Why hunt deer from a tree? One reason is because the prevailing wind at 15 or 20 feet above ground will, to a certain extent, distribute human scent over a wider area and above the predominant ground level air currents. This will place a portion or all of the human odor above a whitetail at close range, but it doesn't negate the fact that any deer approaching from downwind will probably pick up your scent at 100 or 150 yards. This means that treestand hunters must, as must ground blind hunters, situate the stand downwind of where deer will appear. If a hunter doesn't know where deer will come from in a specific area then he has no business hunting that location.

Another reason hunters favor treestands over the ground blinds is because their movement is slightly less obvious at close range. This doesn't mean a tree hunter can move his arms like he's waving the American flag on July 4th during a parade, but it does mean small movements (when a deer is within 15 yards) are less likely to be detected if a hunter is in a tree rather than on the ground. Some bowhunters need this edge, but many do not. Many know when to move.

Another reason hunters favor elevated positions is because it gives them a greater visibility over the entire hunting area. My objection is, just how much area does a deer hunter need to cover? Must he be able to see 200 yards in all directions, and pinpoint the movements of deer 100 yards away?

The argument for greater visibility is invalid, in my opinion. I feel the only area a bow or gun hunter must be able to see is nearby, i.e., that range in which he can effectively shoot and kill a whitetail deer with bow or firearm. Anything more is a waste.

If you are 30 feet up a dead popple 75 yards away, or facing the wrong direction in a wide-open birch tree 10 yards away, the buck might just as well be on Mars as where he is. If you can't shoot, you can't shoot, and that is both your fault and your problem.

Kay Richey knew when to move in her treestand. She shot this fine 6-point buck at 10 yards from a low stand.

Claude Pollington shot this buck from an elevated ladder-platform. He waits with another arrow nocked in case the animal gets up, but it didn't.

The third reason some deer huners prefer a treestand is because it allows them to hunt brushy areas when there are varying wind patterns. Such locations offer too many problems for a ground hunter, and many times they are rejected in favor of better spots. Thick, heavy brush is one example. Heavy cover, such as the edge of a cattail swamp, is another. Pin oak flats covered with water in southern states is a third. Wherever you live, whitetails often will inhabit areas where it's impossible to see through, and even more difficult to thread an arrow or bullet through.

It's taken years, but I've overcome my fear of falling. I'm still not crazy about hunting from great heights, but if a treestand is positioned 20 feet or less off the ground I can get comfortable, and with luck, shoot a buck passing by.

Jacqui Nathan uses a treestand to elevate her above heavy brush which would otherwise conceal deer. She tries a shot here.

Treestands come in all shapes and sizes, and at different heights from the ground. I've sat in willow trees which sway 5 feet in either direction when the wind blows softly, and I've stood in other stands in dead popples which I felt would topple if an ant sneezed near its base.

Some treestands are elaborate affairs with railings, padded seats and visibility in all directions. These seldom pay off on public hunting lands. The better elevated platforms are simple rigs with narrow ranges of fire but good cover.

Good cover. What does that mean? It means anything which will conceal hunter movements at close range, and allows a shot in one or two directions only. A treestand hunter need not be able to shoot in all directions—only one or two at the most. If the stand is positioned properly, and downwind from where deer are expected, the hunter need consider only one direction. If you're hunting with a bow consider 30 yards a maximum, and possibly 75 to 100 yards for a rifle. Don't try to cover the landscape from a treestand. It's impossible.

Treestands should be positioned in much the same locations as ground blinds. The only difference—they are elevated and visibility over a wider area is greatly increased. Look for locations downwind from where deer normally travel. Trails leading to and from bedding or feeding areas are good bets, but don't overlook trails leading to an active primary scrape. Bucks often will follow a major or minor travel trail until they get within 100 yards of a fresh and active scrape, and then begin to circle to check downwind for deer or human activity. A treestand located downwind of the point where bucks veer off and begin circling can be a hotspot for a trophy hunter.

A question frequently heard is: How high should a treestand be? Skilled hunters like Claude Pollington often hunt at heights of 35 or 40 feet. I'm surprised they don't have nose bleeds or fainting spells from breathing thin air. For all intents and purposes the ideal treestand should be about 15 feet. Some of my hunting buddies have scored from stands only 8 feet off the ground, and others sit perched on a stand at 18 or 20 feet. Twenty feet would be the maximum in most cases where the tree being used is rather open, and 10 to 12 feet is fine in bushy trees or early in the season when foliage is heavy.

The lower the treestand, the less of an angle for a bow hunter. A bow hunter must shoot at an extreme angle if the deer is close to his tree. As the deer moves farther away, the angle decreases, regardless of treestand height, and the easier the shot (within reason).

A common fault of many treestand hunters is they snuggle up so close to a game trail that incoming or outgoing deer can spot their movement as they prepare to shoot. It's better to situate a treestand 20 to 25 yards from an active trail, and select a tree which has nearby trees to camouflage your position when you decide to shoot. A favorite treestand site of a Missouri buddy is in a clump of five trees growing from a single trunk. He must turn his body slightly to shoot around one or the other tree trunks, but the heavy screening of nearby trees prevents deer from seeing him. He collects his buck each year, and never has to look for another site.

Wide open or bushy trees? Another question treestand hunters ask, and a good one which bears investigation.

All things being equal, most veteran treestand users would prefer a bushy tree over an open one. Open treestand sites offer unlimited maneuverability, good visibility and a clean field of fire. But is that what a deer hunter really needs? I think not. It's my belief that bushy trees are best providing the hunter removes just enough foliage or limbs to offer a clear shot at whitetails moving through the area. Never deface a tree, and do not remove all limbs even on private property, but judiciously prune away a few offenders so a bow can be drawn or rifle lifted into shooting position. Keep the tree full and natural looking, and this will prevent approaching whitetails from spotting movement.

Position treestands so a right-handed hunter can swing left to shoot, or a southpaw can swing right to shoot. Little nubs, limbs or twigs can be removed to prevent making noise as bow or gun is lifted into position for the shot.

A treestand must be comfortable. If not, the hunter is placed in the awkward posi-

Situate a treestand 20–25 yards from an active deer trail instead of snuggling up tight to the path. You can get a better shot from that position, and the deer is less apt to spot your movement.

This hunter has positioned his treestand so he can swing around for a shot. He uses the treetrunk for a rest to steady his aim.

tion of having to continually move to relieve a crick in his back, neck or lower extremities. The stand should be level, impossible to move from side to side, and offer firm support for the hunter. Nothing is worse than being 20 feet up a tree in a stand that wobbles, teeters or shakes in the faintest breeze.

A comfortable treestand means more than a stable platform. Many hunters, including myself, favor a seat that is firm, with the back against the treetrunk and the feet planted on the floor. Such rigs are easily prepared, and allow the sportsman the maximum comfort in a tree while relieving strain on back and legs. Many folks sit on portable tree stands with legs hanging over the edge; this reduces circulation to legs and feet and raises the possibility of an accident. Numb, tingly gone-to-sleep legs are hazards when climbing down from a treestand.

It's a good idea for any treestand hunter to use a safety strap. Make sure the strap is properly and safely anchored around the treetrunk and around your waist. Safety belts can save your life.

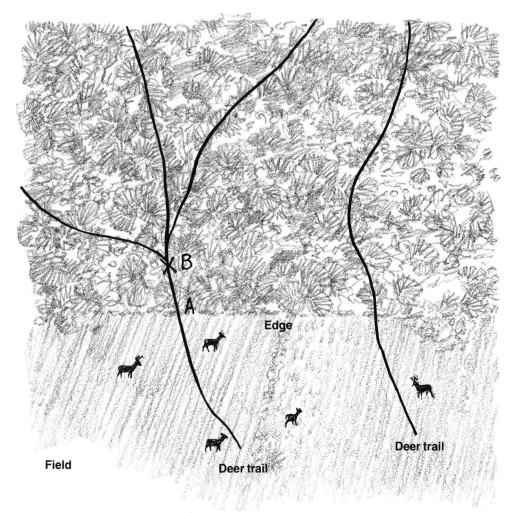

Position treestands away from the edge of a field. You'll see more deer from a field-edge stand (A), but you'll shoot more deer from a position in a wooded area where two or more trails converge (B).

A common fault of many beginning deer hunters is they wish to sit at the edge of a field or huge feeding area where deer can be seen in all directions. This enables the hunter to see deer daily, but it precludes the opportunity for many shots.

For optimum performance, a treestand should be positioned inside the wooded area through which whitetails move to reach the feeding site. How far inside is anyone's guess, but a minimum of 50 yards appears best. One hundred yards from the feeding area is good providing the hunter can position the stand downwind from approaching deer.

Deer often move from bedding to feeding areas via different routes, and these trails may resemble the frayed ends of a rope. But, they often meet to form one or possibly two main trails leading from heavy cover to the dinner table. The best spot for a treestand is 20 to 25 yards downwind from where the minor trails converge into a major trail being used by deer.

Veteran deer hunters know fringeland bucks often follow faint trails which parallel major trails used by does, fawns and immature bucks. Look sharp to locate these buck trails, and again position your treestand downwind from these locations. Just make certain that being downwind of one trail does not blow your scent into the path being used by does and fawns. If these animals get your scent the ballgame will be over as they run off snorting and blowing. Any buck within hearing distance will spook, and the hunter can write off that location for the day. Deer occasionally come back after being spooked, but often by another route.

Deer hunters must constantly work around shifting air currents. Even when the prevailing wind is from one direction, a storm front moving in or out of an area can cause the wind to swirl or change directions. The savvy treestand hunter will have two or three sites in mind to cope with wind-direction changes.

In hilly or mountainous areas hunters must cope with air thermals morning and evening in addition to wind direction. Warming air in mountain valleys moves uphill and carries scent with it in the morning, and the reverse is true in the late afternoon and evening as cooling air forces the scent back down the hill or mountain.

Treestand hunters in such areas learn to anticipate these changes, and place their stands above or below deer runways to prevent an animal from whiffing human scent. A Puff Bottle of unscented powder is handy to carry, and a little squirt of powder will indicate wind direction and to a lesser extent thermal movements.

Ground blind or treestand? Each can be extremely productive for a deer hunter, and the misuse of either method can ruin a deer hunt. Both can be prime spots from which to shoot a buck providing the hunter does his homework by studying food sources and terrain features.

CHAPTER 5

Ten Ambush Sites
for Bucks

Show me a fringeland whitetail buck, and I'll show you an animal that can be taken by a skilled hunter. Note the word "skilled," because there is a tremendous difference between being skilled and lucky.

True, a hunter may shuffle out into the corner cornfield, choose a spot that looks good and dump a buck with trophy antlers. This happens each year, but it doesn't occur often enough for many of us to develop a friendly relationship with Lady Luck. A knowledge of deer food, habitat, terrain requirements and hunting techniques are far better tools for the hunter.

There beats within the heart of every deer hunter a desire to learn how and where to ambush deer—to find a spot where success is a sure thing, and where year after year he can take a nice buck.

This chapter will point out several areas where antlered whitetails can be taken with regularity. That's right, year after year after year. A buck a year is possible from these spots providing hunter pressure doesn't chase the animals away, foods do not change or the habitat and terrain features are not altered.

These locations are not magical places where antlered whitetails stand in place apparently oblivious to everything around them as a hunter blazes away. The locations are common wherever fringeland whitetails are found, but the mix of all necessary ingredients must be present before they become genuine hotspots.

It's up to you to determine whether all necessary factors are present before the hunt begins. You must study all available data on the area long before the season opens.

I'm a firm believer that nothing exceeds a farmland whitetail buck for savvy. They are born and raised near humans, and those animals which have survived for two or more years are crafty. They know how to avoid human contact, and their life depends on instinctive reactions.

The following list of hotspots only work if you understand enough about whitetails to know when and why they use such locations. The areas I'll discuss are survival locations; places where a whitetail buck will go when pressure gets heavy. They produce because we must depend on other hunters to force the buck to be there when you want him.

Big bucks grow old by being a tad bit luckier than their cousins, and by learning valuable lessons early in life. Increased noise on opening day (even before daybreak) is enough to send wallhanger bucks heading for cover long before the first pink light of dawn creases the eastern horizon.

Hunters, unfortunately, are their own worst enemy. Deer hunters are gregarious souls, and they babble away when they get out of the car. They slam car doors and shine flashlights as they stumble over unfamiliar terrain on the way to the deer blind they built the day before. Will a whitetail buck hang around to see what all the opening-day commotion is about? Not hardly. He will go into hiding and venture out only under cover of darkness. The bigger and older (wiser) bucks will feed close to a remote bedding location, and go through hunting season without showing themselves.

Noise, human conversation and human scent are disturbing to deer. It makes them move early, and seek out a safe thicket where humans never go.

Learn to know where bucks will go, and use the wind to your advantage while allowing other hunters to move deer to you. It requires footwork and common sense to determine whether each of the following locations offers what you need, and what a big buck needs, and it also means leaving hunting friends behind.

Solitary hunting doesn't appeal to many whitetail hunters for reasons I could never understand. Robert Ruark's famous Old Man once said: "One boy is all boy, two boys is half a boy and three boys is no boy at all."

Now, the old man was talking about teenage boys goofin' off instead of working, and I'm talking about deer hunters. But Ruark's statement has merit. To paraphrase him: one hunter is all hunter, two hunters is half a hunter and three hunters is no hunter at all.

Two hunters make twice as much noise as one, and distribute twice as much scent over an area. They also require twice as much room to hunt in, and many topnotch ambush sites are just right for one person. Three hunters simply compound the existing problem, and what may have been a superb location for one is ruined by trying to find enough room where three can hunt together.

Gregariousness is fine at church, weddings and family reunions but it falls short when a hunter is working an ambush site. Learn the joys of solitary hunting, and learn to be dependent on your own actions and judgments. Take leave of hunting buddies, or work with them on other techniques where a larger group of warm bodies is needed, but hunt ambush sites alone. It may sound difficult, but the results are worth the effort.

One hunt was a turning point in my deer-hunting career. It taught me the value of solitary hunting, and I learned the importance of knowing how and where to locate one-man ambush sites.

This hunter likes to bowhunt during gun season, and he prefers hunting alone. An ambush site works best for one person. Less noise, scent and commotion.

It was the fifth day of Michigan's sixteen-day firearms deer season, and many hunters had given up. I'd been busy the first four days of the hunt helping friends and relatives get their buck, and now the woods seemed as empty of whitetails as my freezer was of venison.

Two days earlier I had watched a nice eight-point buck sneak through the brush in an area I'd never hunted. The brush was a narrow finger of gray dogwood along an abandoned fencerow. I'd never seen a buck or doe use this area, but it did lead into a thick cedar swamp where whitetails bedded down. It was logical that the faint trail was an escape route used only in times of danger. The trail wasn't bold and wide like other whitetail trails I'd seen, and it obviously wasn't an area frequented by large numbers of deer. On close examination, it turned out to be an escape route used by just one buck, and only when he was pressured to get to thick cover.

Bright and early the next day I plunked my fanny down 50 yards downwind from the faint trail. Two hours passed without sign of a deer. I was dreaming of coffee and a hot danish when the clatter and racket of car doors slamming drifted downwind to me on the freshening breeze. It sounded like a riot in progress. It was getting late in the season, and obviously a group of hunters was planning a drive in hopes of moving a buck past someone. All thoughts of coffee slipped away as the hunters began moving my way in noisy fashion.

Several does and fawns squirted out ahead of the hunters as the animals headed for the security of the nearby swamp. The drivers had posted two standers near the swamp, but they overlooked the tiny sliver of thick cover entering the swamp. That was just fine with me because I had it covered, and they didn't know another hunter was in the area. Neither did the buck I'd been looking for.

The buck was cool in the face of danger. He came slinking like an antlered snake along the thick dogwood tangle with his head held low in a semi-crouch. He would take a few steps, pause momentarily and look over his shoulder at the approaching drivers before moving again. Each stop was a study in animal concentration. He used the available cover to his advantage. Evidently he had used this escape route before, and had never encountered any problems. He really wasn't expecting any as he approached within 50 yards of my position.

The wind was blowing from him to me, and since my position in the fencerow provided cover the buck didn't know I had him covered. I settled the Weaver crosshairs low behind his front shoulder, and admired him for a moment before taking the shot.

As the rifle roared the buck stumbled, caught his balance and continued at a dead run along the dogwood for another 50 yards before his legs quit moving and he folded up. I was punching holes in my firearms tag before tying it to his antlers when one of the deer drivers approached. He wanted to know why I'd been sitting there.

"Bucks always head directly into the cedar swamp," he said. "This is the first time I've seen deer move along this dogwood swale."

"It may be the first time you've seen deer move through here," I responded, "but that's only because you've fallen into a rut of driving the area the same way. Each year you push this spot, and each time a buck slips out ahead of the drivers and you never get a shot."

I told him that many bucks, particularly larger animals, often have escape routes they use in times of danger. The big bucks seldom follow the lead of does, fawns or smaller bucks, but prefer to use a little-known trail off to one side which enables them to work back into heavy cover without exposing themselves.

That ol' boy shook his head, muttered something about "luck" and wandered off to join his buddies. He didn't take time to study the escape route, and he didn't learn anything from the experience. The following year I shot another buck in the same location, and the drive contained the same hunters.

"You again, huh?" he muttered as I gutted my buck.

"Yep."

"Got lucky again, eh?"

"Yep."

I'm a man of few words when hunters won't listen to reason.

The following pages should generate some thought on ambush sites. It should stir up memories, and questions. Some folks have spent a lifetime studying whitetail deer, and they often can spot an ambush site just like a professional photographer can spot that perfect picture.

Ambush sites fall into several categories, and here's the first.

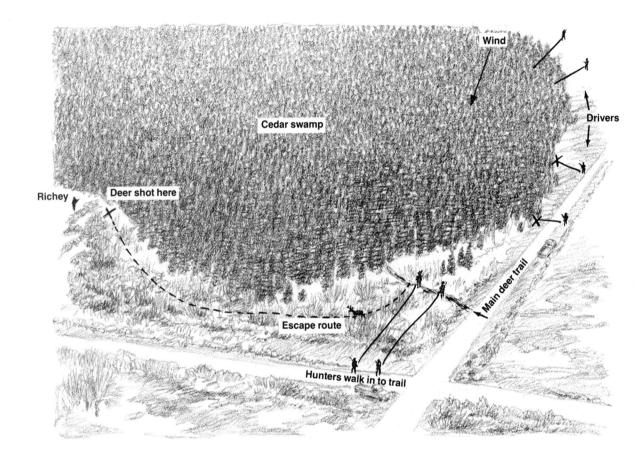

The drivers had posted two standers near the swamp. I took my stand in a tiny sliver of thick cover at the entrance. Unwittingly, the drivers pushed the buck straight toward me along an escape route that led into the swamp.

Escape Routes

Escape routes, those little-used deer trails favored by big bucks when the going gets tough, are hard to find. In many cases they will parallel a heavily used game trail, but often will be found in thicker cover. A bent blade of grass, a broken twig or an occasional footprint may be the only clue you'll have to the existence of such trails.

The key to locating these trails is to know where deer bed down during the day and where they travel to feed. Escape routes often will be found nearby, and frankly, it requires plenty of searching to find them. Conduct a hands-and-knees examination for 50 yards on each side of a well used trail, and you may get lucky.

One trail I found didn't reveal itself to me until one hand and a knee was in the middle of the indistinct path. A fall mushroom was growing, and I studied it for a moment before everything started clicking into place. There, beside the mushroom, was the splayed track of a big deer. I inched forward, looked in the direction of travel and spotted a bracken fern sharply indented from a deer's foot. Five feet farther along I could see another track, but a person would have to be really looking hard to spot the trail. It didn't look like it had been used for weeks, but it was an escape route through heavy cover.

I followed the trail on hands and knees, and it led through a narrow sumac thicket while the main deer trail skirted the tangle. Fifty yards farther on it sneaked through a seemingly impenetrable wall of dogwood and on into a tiny stub of thick cedar swamp which connected with the large main body of swamp.

This is it, I thought excitedly. This is where a buck can be shot. The escape route is the key because it offers heavy cover for a nervous buck to use between feeding and bedding areas, and it should produce on opening day.

I stood up and surveyed the terrain. I lowered my profile to the level used by a buck, and looked again. The animal would be hidden from view of hunters manning the main trail 40 yards away, and the buck could pass through to the swamp without being seen.

Now came the hard part. I had to figure out where to sit in order to ambush the buck on opening day.

I had to study the wind. Fortunately, I knew the prevailing wind direction in the area. I then had to find an area which would be downwind and within shooting range of the escape route. After spending three hours scouring the area, only one spot came to mind. The tiny wedge of tangled cedars that connected to the main body of the swamp was my logical choice because it offered a place to hide. One cedar had fallen in a windstorm, and the maze of roots provided a backrest and concealment behind me. It looked like a natural, but I wanted to be sure.

I placed a dead tree limb in a horizontal position 3 feet above ground between two cedars. This would be the approximate height of a buck's back as he moved down the escape route. Then I paced the distance from the trail to the cedar roots, and it was 35 yards.

Good, good. Now it was necessary to sit with my back to the roots and see if the limb could be seen.

No, dammit, other cedars blocked my view of the trail. I moved the limb 10 feet down the trail, and tried again. No dice.

I moved the dead limb halfway in between the first and second locations, sat down and looked. The limb was barely visible through the wall of cedar trees.

I had my spot.

The next time I saw the escape route was two months later on opening day. Hunters were all around me, but they were evenly spaced along the well-used game trail leading into the swamp. I entered my blind from downwind an hour before sunup, sat down quietly with my knees up in front and my Ruger .44 Magnum braced against my shoulder.

I wanted a heavy bullet with tremendous shocking power for the short-range shot. When and if a buck appeared he would be visible for only an instant, and I suspected he wouldn't show himself until several minutes after the shooting started on the main deer trail. I suspected he would hold back, allow other deer to filter down the trail and run into the hunters.

I was right. Ten minutes after daybreak a small herd of young bucks and does came along the main trail, and the shooting started. Then the yelling began.

"Get one, Joe?" someone yelled 100 yards away.

"I hit him, and he ran your way," came the reply.

It was followed by two more shots, and the noise of a hunter moving through the brush. Another shot, and then just the faint murmur of happy conversation. Someone had scored on a small buck.

The shots and conversation registered on my brain, but I kept my attention riveted to the escape route. If a buck was coming he'd be along any moment.

Long, white antler tines showed like the winking of headlights far away on a dark night as the buck pussyfooted through heavy cover along his escape route. I could see the antlers for a second, and then they disappeared as he stepped behind another cedar.

I slowly raised the .44 Mag off my knees, rested my cheek against the stock and stared at the dead limb which was still in place. Within moments the buck would be in position for a shot, and I had to be ready to flip the safety off. Two or three seconds was all I'd have before the animal would be screened again.

First the nose and then the eye and antlers came into view. The buck paused, looked away at the unheard commotion apparently going on as the other hunters relived the kill. Then the buck made his move.

The safety went off without conscious thought, and as the buck's neck came into view I stroked the trigger. The nine-point buck went down in a heap, and never regained his feet.

I didn't move for sixty minutes. The other hunters had heard the shot, but I didn't want them to know where I had been sitting or where the escape route was located. It's just one way of keeping your hunting area intact.

Never draw attention, if possible, to the location of your hunting position near an escape route. Sneak in and sneak out, and if necessary tag the deer, walk out to the car, drop off your firearm and return for the animal after dark. The anecdote at the beginning of this chapter proves it's not always possible to keep the area a secret, but in many cases other hunters will just feel you were lucky to be in the right place at the right time. Never discourage that feeling.

Escape routes are not easy to find, but look for them in thick cover off to one side of a main trail. Once you find one, and determine wind direction and where you can see to shoot, you'll take a fringeland buck.

Snow-Covered Cornfields

Earlier in this book I described a hunt for a big buck in a snow-covered cornfield. We didn't score that time, but since then I've learned how and when to hunt the corn.

The trick is fundamental, but it often eludes many hunters in northern climes where tracking snow conditions are as much a part of the hunt as blaze-orange clothing. Whitetail deer in fringeland areas eat corn once snow covers other food, and a standing cornfield is a late-season magnet for deer.

The only thing to remember about hunting corn is that does and fawns generally are the first animals to come to feed. Bucks follow later, and often move to the grain during the last minutes of daylight. If legal shooting time in your hunting area ends before dark ... well, ignore this tip and proceed to the next one.

The important thing about hunting corn is knowing where the animals feed. A cornfield may be a mile square, but deer generally will feed in one small area. They will feed there until food runs out, and then move to another nearby location often only 50 yards away.

Locate the feeding site, and construct a natural blind from corn stalks. Make it small, keep it natural and be sure it is downwind from the feeding area. Check the proposed area of your blind for deer tracks in the snow; it doesn't pay to construct a cornstalk blind only to find whitetails moving upwind into your scent stream. Police the area well, and select a downwind location where deer do not travel. It may be slightly farther from the feeding zone than one would like, but what's a hunter going to do?

Ideally, the blind should be within 50 yards of the feeding site. Break down a few cornstalks to provide a shooting lane, and enter your blind from downwind. Play the wind like a fine instrument, and keep it in your face at all times.

It may mean cold hunting, but gunning cornfields places heavy emphasis on being able to sit still. Several hunters I know hunt the corn each year during gun season, and each one manages a nice buck.

"But, it can be colder than hell," states one buddy.

"It also means being able to sit motionless for two or three hours," another corn hunter says. "If cold and immobility are two things you can't handle then you're better off moving through the woods with other hunters."

Then he snickered because he knows these hunters would push deer to him for a close shot as animals leave heavy cover to feed at dusk.

Whitetails feed in standing corn during late fall and through the winter because it

These fringeland hunters know a secret: deer feed only in one small portion of a cornfield at a time. So they built a blind nearby. This buck was shot at dawn as it fed back to its bed.

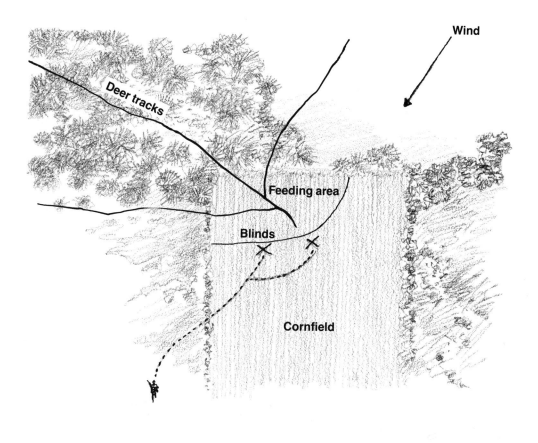

Construct a cornstalk blind downwind from the general feeding area where whitetails congregate. This ambush site is one of the best, provided the hunter can walk to his blind without disturbing the area.

offers a good food supply and cover. It's not uncommon to watch deer filter into the corn along a maze of trails, but these trails almost always lead to the dinner table. A downwind blind along one of the corn trails is an alternate selection although the hunter must forever be cognizant of other animals moving behind him. One hint of hunter scent, and the hunt will be over for that day. And rest assured that on subsequent days the whitetails will remember your position, and be ever cautious during their approach to feed.

Drainage Ditches

A drainage ditch, dry creekbed or any deep, narrow depression in fringeland country can be an excellent place to harvest a buck during hunting season. Bucks, and to a lesser degree does and fawns, travel these natural terrain features whenever danger threatens. Some hunters have learned their value, but many have not.

One year I was hunting red foxes in southern Michigan farmland. The Walker hounds jumped a fox in a slashing, and hazed the animal back and forth through a large woodlot for thirty minutes.

This hunter walks a narrow depression in fringeland country. He knows whitetail bucks often use such areas. Thick brush nearby offers good deer cover.

This trophy deer shot by Paul Mickey is Michigan's largest nontypical whitetail. It often used a drainage ditch for a travel route.

I knew red foxes often traveled the drainage ditch that cut diagonally across the section. The ditch was 6 feet deep, and a tiny trickle of water flowed through it during warm weather. It was ice-covered and slippery now, but on many occasions I had killed a dog fox in midwinter as he tried to escape the hounds by running the ice.

I took up a station 50 yards from the woodlot and waited just around a tiny bend in the ditch. The hounds were pounding my way, and I felt Big Red would soon come into sight.

My jaw dropped open when a buck with one remaining antler skidded around the corner, spotted me and slid to a stop 10 yards away. He crawled and scampered up from the ditch, and was last seen taking a hasty exit through the nearby field.

Deer season was closed, and deer-running hounds are worthless to fox hunters. I grabbed a hefty stick and belabored hell out of the dogs when they came boohooing around the bend.

That incident proved that under stress bucks will use drainage ditches or creekbeds for travel when they have their backs to the wall from hunter pressure. Paul Mickey's big buck (discussed in an earlier chapter) used a ditch for a travel route, and many other bucks do the same.

A ditch or creekbed should have some cover. Barren, wide-open ditches are seldom good because they offer little protection for a moving animal and spooky bucks will choose other escape routes. Ideally, a ditch will have cattails, tag alder or sumac growing inside it, and it will not have much water. A jump-across stream is just right. The ditch should have heavy cover within 200 yards on either side, and it must be thick and located close to the ditch. A hardpressed buck like the one being chased by our foxhounds took to the open fields once he spotted me but had I been located elsewhere he would have continued on 100 yards and exited into a thick woodlot adjoining the ditch.

Adjoining woodlots, swales, marshes or other heavy cover should have immediate covered access from the ditch. Look for a tiny sliver of woods which leaves a woodlot and enters the drainage ditch, and check out any brushy fencerows which connect the ditch with other cover. A buck generally will leave a woodlot at the first hint of danger, enter a drainage ditch and proceed until he comes to an exit where he has enough available cover to conceal his movements into another woodlot.

Each drainage ditch or creekbed is different, and must be hunted with common sense. Select a site to sit downwind from any thick cover which enters or leaves the ditch. Do not sit fully exposed at the top of the ditch unless some available cover offers concealment, but sit down in the ditch near the junction where the fencerow or finger of woods meets the drainage ditch. A buck will follow the cover until he reaches the comparative safety of the ditch, pause for a moment and continue on his way. Be prepared for fast shots at close range.

Evergreen Plantations or Christmas Tree Farms

Hunters in northern states have known for years that evergreen plantations or Christmas tree farms are hotspots for snowshoe hares. The hares find food, cover and protection from overhead predation in such thickets. Whitetail bucks in fringeland areas of this country seldom fear overhead predation. They do, however, seek protection from the elements and from hunting pressure. Bucks often hole up in such areas.

Evergreen plantations are thick, and nearly impenetrable in some areas. The thicker and more difficult they are for hunters to move through, the more attractive they are for bucks. Mind you, big expansive tracts are not necessarily better for deer-hunting purposes. A small, compact plantation measuring only 10 acres is plenty big enough to harbor a trophy whitetail buck.

Do not confuse Scotch pine, spruce and balsam plantations with a cedar swamp. Swamps are low-lying areas while most evergreen plots are located high and dry. The ideal location for a plantation hunting site is where the evergreens connect with a swamp on one side via some type of brushy cover and cropland or upland hardwoods on another. Nearby food is important, and a spillover of whitetails often occurs between the swamp and the plantation. Does, fawns and lesser bucks will hole up in the swamp when the redcoats arrive, but a savvy buck will disappear into a plantation faster than your weekly paycheck when hunters start moving around. Once inside, a big buck is tough to find and harder to hunt. He's difficult to move out during a drive because he can dodge behind an evergreen 20 feet away, and never be seen. One can try still-hunting, moving a step at a time, and spend more time looking than walking, but that age-old technique seldom works with fringeland whitetail deer.

Few whitetail bucks move into an evergreen plantation until after hunting season opens. When hunters are on the move, and noise or pressure from bowhunters increases, a buck heads for cover like a woodchuck jumping into his meadow hole. A big buck can be as happy as a clam at high tide with 10 acres of evergreens providing cover.

The trick to taking bucks from evergreen plantations is to be there before the buck decides to do his vanishing act. Bucks often move into such areas on opening day when the shooting starts, often before dawn. They get a jump on the hunters, and will be firmly ensconced deep in the thicket before most hunters enter nearby woods.

Hunters who wish to take a pine-plantation buck must locate the most probable route he will take to gain safety. This can be accomplished long before hunting season opens. Look for brushy fencerows leading from nearby feeding areas or adjacent wood-lots into the evergreen plantation. Locate a natural depression like a gulley between two rolling hills which contacts the evergreens. Find any terrain feature that can offer cover to a moving buck as he seeks sanctuary in the pines. Such areas leading from feeding or wooded sites to heavy cover are seldom used except on opening day.

Once you've scouted the area, and located the main travel lanes used by a buck searching for a place to hide, you have to find the best place to ambush him. Mature whitetail bucks generally approach a pine plantation upwind. They will wind-check the area before committing themselves to the move, and this means you have to be downwind from the probable entrance site. The ideal ambush site will be inside the plantation, and downwind from the route taken by the buck when he makes his move. Such areas generally have thick cover which means short shots. Those who score often shoot bucks at 20 yards or less.

Such close-range shooting indicates the need for a masking scent. I use a skunk scent to mask my odor. Too much skunk scent, of course, amounts to overkill, but a few drops on nearby leaves or on the ground near your stand are good insurance. They may prevent an errant breeze from washing your scent into the path of a nice buck.

Work into the hunting area from downwind, and be in position one hour before sun-up if the law permits. Your preselected location should be easy to find, and it should be on the ground with a good back rest to break up your silhouette. Use a thin veil of cover in front of the stand to conceal your movements, but keep it sparse and natural.

The pine-plantation hunter depends more on sitting still and allowing the animal to

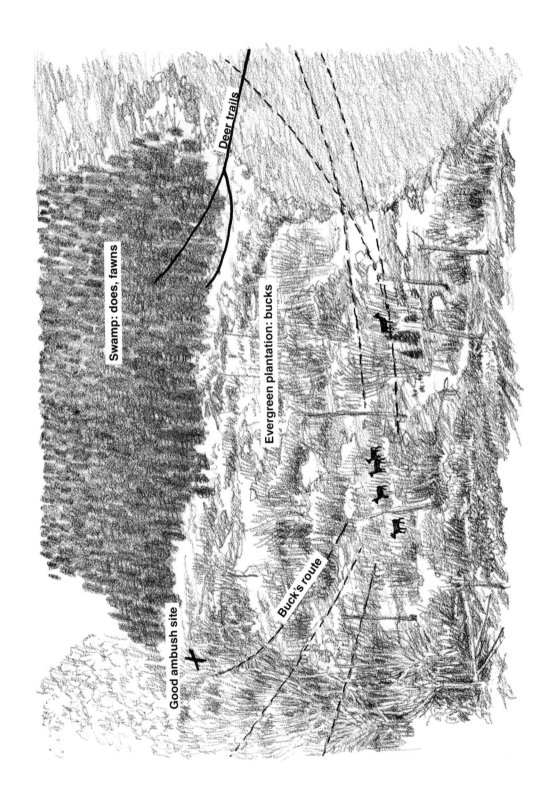

Swamp: does, fawns

Deer trails

Evergreen plantation: bucks

Buck's route

Good ambush site

Opposite: Look for an ambush site where an evergreen plantation butts up against a cedar swamp, feeding area and hardwoods. The best spot is any thick brush which connects the evergreens with a feeding area.

Masking scent can help neutralize human odor. I use skunk scent sparingly on my boots, and on the ground nearby.

come to him than he does on being able to see long distances. A buck will often move into the evergreen plantation, and then stop to survey his backtrail before moving deeper into cover. This pause, which may last from five seconds to a minute, offers the ideal time to take the shot. Take your shot as the buck checks things out behind him, and if your hunting site was chosen with care you'll be dining on fresh venison liver that evening.

Cedar Swamps

Cedar swamps are hotspots for whitetail hunters. Swamps are difficult to hunt because they are hard to get into and out of. Shoot a buck in a swamp, and you'll soon learn the true meaning of masochism. Self-inflicted pain walks hand in hand with swamp hunting. Only the most dedicated hunter is willing to drag a buck from a cedar tangle after a long hunting day.

Such locations offer an excellent chance to ambush a buck. These areas offer deer as much protection as a bomb shelter, and they attract only a few hardy hunters each year. Few people wish to wade through water to find a spot to hunt, and the thought of getting lost is enough to turn off many people.

Deer frequent these areas because they are looking for a way to avoid human contact during hunting season. Swamps offer little in the way of food, but they do offer protection from the elements and hunter pressure. For this reason a swamp can be a good place to hunt during firearms season.

We've noted how human sound, hunter noise and an increase in human odor in fields and woods send whitetail deer into hiding. Let's now look at how those deer enter a swamp, and how to choose the best place to wait on stand.

Increased activity on opening day is sure to drive any bucks into the relative safety of a cedar swamp. Thick tangled brush, low-hanging cedars and knee-deep water pose few problems for a buck, but they can make the two-legged hunter pause for thought before he enters such an area.

The savvy hunter knows a whitetail will stand in water for hours if need be to avoid detection, but deer—like hunters—generally prefer some comfort. Although they'll wade through water to reach safety, deer prefer being high and dry.

When preseason scouting in a cedar swamp, look for high, dry areas. A slightly thicker stand of dry cover in the middle of a swamp often will be the preferred site for a wise old buck to wile away hunting season. Look for big tracks in the soft earth, and signs of bedding areas. Consider other nearby areas within the swamp where a buck could seek cover.

An old hunting buddy once told me: "Everyone knows big bucks—the so-called 'swamp bucks'—head for thick cover as soon as hunters start shooting outside the swamp. What they don't know is how to get into and out of the swamp without being winded by deer!

"I use a canoe to work into the swamps," he said. "Many swamps have a stream flowing through them, and a canoe allows the solitary hunter to travel at his own pace. Slow sculling with a paddle can ease a small canoe silently through a thick swamp, and allow detailed examination of potential bedding sites."

He paddles along until he spots a dry hummock within the swamp. Preseason scouting offers him the opportunity to check the hummock for fresh sign, old spoor and old tracks that indicate the area could be used for a hideaway during hunting season.

"Many times I've sneaked into a swamp with my camouflaged canoe, pulled it up within shooting range of the hummock, and been in hunting position by daybreak," he said. "I make sure I'm downwind of the area being hunted, and often will sit in my canoe. A few cedar branches placed over the canoe and behind me serves to break up my silhouette, and then it's just a matter of waiting for the buck to show.

"Some years a buck will amble through swamp water to the dry hummock, turn around once or twice like a dog before a warm fire, and then settle down. I try to shoot them before they lie down."

This deer hunter sits in a tangled cedar swamp, waiting for an opening-day buck to appear on the dry hummock.

The technique sounds simple, and it sure beats hell out of wading on foot through the swamp. Hipboots or waders are a must if the swamp is filled with water, but a canoe should be used whenever possible to work into the area. A whitetail may jump or swim a small stream, but canoe travel will allow the hunter to travel without leaving his scent behind for a moving buck to discover.

Locate the swamp, use a canoe to travel by water into the middle of it, find a bedding area nearby and be ready to shoot. It's easy!

Small Woodlots

A teeny-tiny woodlot in the back forty often serves as a hideout for fringeland bucks. Because it seems too small to harbor deer it may go unhunted. Hunters should check out these locations with bow or gun.

Some years ago the aforementioned John McKenzie and I would scout small woodlots in early October. We didn't know it then, but we were passing up some fine bow-hunting. Our intention was to scout bucks in anticipation of Michigan's sixteen-day firearms season which traditionally opens November 15. We looked for buck rubs, scrapes, tracks in soft earth near croplands, and we looked for and found bedding areas. All puzzle pieces were put together into what we called The Game Plan for implementation on opening day.

Look to teeny-tiny woodlots for fringeland bucks. Rock star Ted Nugent did, and collected this nice 8-pointer. He knew the buck was using the woodlot so he set up an ambush site nearby.

Claude Pollington guessed right on this buck and shot it from an ambush site. This is the man Outdoor Life *magazine calls "The Whitetail Wizard."*

We knew that in farmland country where there are few bucks whitetails are like circuit preachers a century ago. They are here today, four miles away the next day, three miles away the third day and back home again on the fourth. We learned that regardless of which mile-square section a buck may be temporarily residing in, he had to pick up the next evening and move to another haunt. These fringeland bucks move day and night when the mood strikes them, and we learned where they crossed dirt roads and we knew which woodlot appealed to their sense of safety. We also learned how to ambush these bucks on opening day. Remember, we did our homework for forty-five days before the season opener and we knew exactly which woodlot would hold bucks. It was a simple chore to pick the right spot to sit so the antlered whitetail would cross in front of our guns.

Here's how we did it. Once we determined which woodlot we felt would harbor bucks on opening day, we would scout it thoroughly. In almost every case a tangle of low-growing berry bushes would serve as a bedding spot for the buck, and almost every time the animal would be in his home bed long before daybreak. Every buck we killed (except one) in woodlots was inside the wooded area before sunup.

We silently positioned one hunter downwind from the bedding area along a trail the deer would use to flee the woodlot. This hunter would be in place one hour before the other man would circle around and walk downwind through the woodlot. The trick was to execute a sneak-drive, and allow the wind to wash hunter scent downwind to the bedding buck.

Seldom would the sneak-driver see the buck as it ghosted from its bed. The animal would hear and smell the hunter moving downwind, leave the safety of its bedding area and begin a dignified retreat along a trail which would lead to another patch of heavy cover. If we guessed right, which we did year after year, the buck would walk right up to the standing hunter.

Narrow Fingers of Woods

We've all seen whitetails in farmland, near heavy cover, feeding in croplands or along acorn ridges. How do these deer move when danger threatens? They move through heavy cover, that's how. Does, fawns and young bucks may skip across a field like first graders heading for school, but larger, more mature bucks with heavy antlers use whatever cover they can find. A narrow finger of woods which connects a woods with another thicker woodlot, or a woods with a nearby swamp, attracts whitetail bucks like road apples draw flies. And small fingers of woods are found everywhere.

Deer often are caught feeding in croplands when opening day rolls around. The smaller ones will dart across open fields in an attempt to gain safety. But not big bucks; they head for safety along routes which offer some degree of protection. A narrow finger of woods which connects with heavy cover in at least two directions is a natural.

Many such areas are brushy, difficult to walk through and offer excellent concealment for deer doing a disappearing act. Avoid woodlot fingers which are open and offer
little cover, and instead choose those with plenty of cover. A buck may use these areas
on opening day and not again until later in the season when hunters start driving. Preseason scouting will tell you which narrow woodlot finger deer will use. Look for old
tracks, droppings, buck rubs or old scrapes.

Select a natural ground blind area or treestand site long before the season opens. Position it downwind from the suspected travel lane being used, and stay away from it
until opening day. As with all preseason scouting, too much human scent in an area
can cause big bucks to abandon the route.

*A short-barreled 12-gauge shotgun was
just the ticket for Paul Kerby, who knew
this 6-point fringeland whitetail was
using the narrow finger of woods in the
background as a travel route. Kerby located a good site to sit downwind from
the trail and collected this buck.*

Most wooded fingers are so narrow you may have to sit with your back to an open field in order to be away from the trail. That's fine providing you're not silhouetted against a barren field. Once I hunted a brush-choked wooded finger that connected two woodlots, and it was so narrow I had to sit in an adjacent cornfield. Several cornstalks pulled down around me served as a natural blind, and the eight-point buck I nailed that year came sneaking along the trail the second day of the season and never suspected I was there.

A hunter isn't bound by law to sit within the narrow finger of woods, and common sense told me that if I tried to squeeze my skinny body into the finger I would spook the animal. Further use of common sense dictated a nearby cornfield blind which overlooked the trail I knew the buck would follow. The corn offered concealment on the downwind side, and an excellent view of the trail.

Such narrow connections between woods, or woods and swamps, are natural avenues of travel for whitetail bucks, and should never be passed over lightly. A hunter may opt for sitting in some thicket where deer trails converge, but I've learned that a woodlot finger used by bucks on a regular basis is better.

Fencerows

The best fencerows are thick and brushy. Often a fence may be down in places, and more often than not it will be grown over with dogwood or some other thick cover. Gaps or gates in the fence and low-growing cover will provide areas a buck can move through as he travels from one patch of thick cover to another.

It's these natural breaks in a fencerow which offer attractive hunting sites for fringeland hunters. A buck under pressure often will follow a thick fencerow. Fencerows often traverse open fields, and the buck can scan the terrain ahead for signs of danger while remaining screened.

A whitetail buck moves in stops and starts, and occasionally will look over or through the thick fencerow to view the terrain on the opposite side. He generally moves into the wind, and often will stop just before a break in the fence or at an open fence gate to check for danger before proceeding.

A hunting buddy of mine kills a buck each year during Ontario's gun season, and he does it along a brush-choked split-rail fence that meanders through an open field between two slashings.

"Each year a buck will pussyfoot along that split-rail fence, take a peeky-boo through a wee gap in the fence and then press on for the slashing," he said. "I sit downwind of the gap where I can watch both sides of the field in a little hide of broken split rails, and each year on opening day a buck will travel the fencerow on the side away from other hunters and walk right up to me."

He seldom has to take long shots at bucks crossing through the opening because years of experience have taught him to sit tight and wait for a buck to appear in the fence's gap. "There have been times when the buck was within 20 yards of me before I saw it, but almost always they hesitate before going through the gap in the fence," he said. "I raise my gun and shoot as they check out distant fields for danger."

Bucks traveling along fencerows seldom jump the fence unless a hunter takes a shot and misses them. They usually follow the fencerow, be it split rail, stone or wire, until they come to a natural opening. These openings act as a funnel for deer and deer hunters. Pick a stand downwind of an opening in the fence. Usually, but not always, deer will move through such openings near heavy cover. They seldom will move through a fencerow in the middle of an open field unless danger threatens; instead, they prefer being close to a swamp or woodlot before they make their move.

Look for a fencerow break within 30 yards of heavy cover. Often a stand can be built just inside the woodlot, and this vantage point will offer concealment in addition to providing a clear view of the fencerow. A buck can be seen for long distances as he moves along a fencerow, and the hunter can pick the spot where he'll take his shot.

Whitetail does often follow fencerows as well. The hunter, if he's gunning for bucks, should be far enough downwind from where the fencerow connects with swamp or woods to allow the does to pass unmolested. Does, fawns and lesser bucks often will precede a large buck down a fencerow, and if these animals catch your scent or see a movement the buck may try to escape across an open field. Sit tight, look sharp and be prepared to pass up lesser animals in hopes of a clean shot at a nice buck.

Hilltops in Open Fields

There's an open field not far from where these words are being written, and each year a buddy of mine takes a nice buck on a hilltop. Sure, there are other hills in the immediate area, but this one produces season after season on opening day.

What would make one hill more productive than another? This particular hill happens to be just a bit higher than the others, and it offers a brushy fencerow 100 yards away in one direction and a narrow finger of woods 100 yards off in another direction. A farm lane cuts across the base of the hill. These natural travel trails are within easy rifle shot of the hilltop.

The nearby hills offer roughly the same options to a hunter but they seldom produce. Only this one hill, as my friend can testify, delivers shots at whitetail bucks booting it for heavy cover on opening day. Each year he will shoot one of the largest bucks taken in the area, and each time the animal is shot at ranges of 40 to 100 yards.

Why? Again, a good question which is difficult to answer. We've both tried to analyze it thoroughly, and we have no logical answer why one hilltop produces while other, nearby hills fail to deliver a single shot at a buck. Perhaps it's that this hill is larger, but other hills offer closer proximity to heavy cover and/or feeding areas. It's just one of those imponderables which we refuse to ponder any longer.

This hilltop overlooks a main road 500 yards away, several open fields and semi-open brushlands within 200 yards. Feeding areas are found within 200 yards, and the balance of the terrain is wide open. Yet, each year my pal kills a nice buck.

The basic question is: Although bucks travel open terrain on opening day under hunter pressure, why do they often travel near the base of high hills?

I've witnessed this phenomenon in many states, and it seems bucks often skirt the highest hill in the area. My buddy's hill rises a scant 200 feet above the mean level of the surrounding terrain, and it can hardly be called a mountain. Nonetheless, bucks seem attracted to the hill as an escape route, and that in itself is good enough for me.

Paul Kerby, the man who kills his buck on the nearby hill each fall, has constructed a tiny blind. It's not elaborate, and it's not pretty like fresh-cut flowers, but it still produces.

"I know that when the sun comes up, and shooting starts nearby, sooner or later a buck will come charging across the open field and pass within 100 yards of my hill," Kerby maintains. "The shots are not easy, and often are at running targets, but if I miss on the first whitetail another buck will be along later."

Open hilltops offer superb views of the immediate area. A spotting scope can be helpful in determining whether distant animals carry antlers or not, but if they are so far away a scope is needed, they are too far away to shoot. The important factor in hunting open hilltops is to remain motionless, and keep a low profile.

"It took me four years of trial and error before I located the perfect hilltop," Kerby said. "I tried several, watching deer at a distance but seldom had a shot. Picking the right hilltop is a lesson in futility at first, but once the correct choice has been made it's easy to score every year."

Whitetails can and will pass near certain hilltops and avoid others. There seems to be no logical reason for this behavior, and it may sound as if an ambush site on a hilltop is a hit-or-miss proposition. And so it is, for a year or a few years, but once the proper location is determined it becomes your private shooting gallery.

A pit blind may be in order. Claude Pollington's Execution Knob is an example of a hilltop which produces year after year. His hilltop features a pit blind, and this effectively reduces his profile and offers a rock-solid shooting platform. Long shots are the rule from hilltops, and the more secure your shooting position, the better chance one has of collecting venison.

This is one ambush site where hunting with others can be productive. If four hilltops are found within a quarter- or half-mile area it behooves the hunters to spread out—one on top of each hill—and learn which spot is best.

A small hilltop can accommodate only one hunter, and he must know the general direction from which bucks appear. The animals generally move at dawn on opening day, and after that the hill is worthless as a hunting site unless one holds an antlerless deer tag. Bucks avoid the area after opening day.

Flat-shooting rifles and light, fast-stepping bullets are used on hilltops. A rifle should be sighted in to shoot 3 inches high at 100 yards, and should hit at point of aim at 250 yards.

This year, if hilltops are a part of your local terrain, try hunting one. Just don't be disappointed if your neighbor takes a nice buck a quarter-mile from your stand; it just may be he knows which hilltop is best. All you can hope for is that he gets sick the following year and can't hunt opening day. Then, you'll have it to yourself.

Cattail Marshes

One year I was hunting ducks in a marsh along Michigan's Saginaw Bay. The area was a maze of tiny potholes surrounded by knee-deep water and cattails. It was a bluebird day, and even the bluebirds weren't flying. I decided to take a hike through the cattails in hopes of jumpshooting a black or mallard before the evening flight occurred.

It was hot. The air was so still I could hear myself sweat. I stumbled over invisible muskrat tunnels, slipped and nearly fell while tripping over underwater hummocks, and never saw a duck.

I was about to chuck the whole mess as a waste of time and energy when a lone drake mallard vaulted from the cattails in a burst of feathers. I swung above the climbing bird, yanked the trigger and caught the drake with a charge of high-base 6s. Down he came, head over curly tail, into a nearby tangle of cattails and algae-dappled water. I waded over to retrieve my bird, and paused to listen to the sound of something wading away from me. I hurried that way, scooped up the drake mallard enroute and wondered whether someone else was hunting the cattail marsh. I'd seen no other hunters, heard no shots and thought I had it to myself.

The sloshing sound of something wading through the water became louder, and as I rounded a thick wall of cattails came almost face to face with a nice buck. The animal was in waist-deep water, and appeared to be having some difficulty moving through the muck.

He studied me, recognized me for what I was and immediately started heaving himself through the water. He blasted through the cattails, and within seconds was out of sight although the sounds of his hasty progress could be heard for several minutes.

Since that day I've run into several bucks using cattail marshes for secret getaway spots. Bow season was in progress at the time of my first encounter, and I suspect the buck had had a narrow escape with a bowman. The animal had taken refuge in a swamp atop a muskrat house, and had I not shot and retrieved the mallard, the buck would have stayed put in relative safety and with scarcely a care in the world.

Paul Mickey, mentioned earlier, once told me about shooting a nice buck in a cattail marsh. The animal had been pushed into the cattails along with other whitetails by hunter pressure, and Mickey happened to see the animals moving through the water. He stalked them, and shot a nice buck.

These bowhunters used a canoe to work back into a cattail marsh, and they scored on a fine buck.

Playing tag with a buck in a thick marsh is not easy, and can lead to heat exhaustion unless you follow a few simple rules.

A deer trail leading to a cattail marsh is the place to start. If sign shows recent travel, and wet entrances or exits from the marsh, it's logical to assume whitetails are using the marsh for a sanctuary. Take up a downwind position in the cattails about 20 yards from the trail. A short stepladder can keep you out of the water while providing an elevated shooting platform. Just remember to stay back in the cattails, and don't move.

Allow moving deer to approach the cattails before taking a shot. Laws vary from state to state, and many prohibit shooting whitetails in the water. This would place the deer in an unfair position, but no state I'm aware of prohibits shooting a buck as it approaches the water. Or, if the buck is leaving the cattail marsh and making his way to dry ground, take the shot as the animal steps from the water.

I've talked with other hunters who successfully stalk bucks in a cattail marsh. They say that a skilled hunter can stalk a whitetail buck by hunting from muskrat house to muskrat house during hunting season. The trick is to move from one area to another into the wind. Gaps in the tops of cattails often reveal small potholes ahead, and muskrat houses often dot the water in these areas. Since tiny mud muskrat houses are dry ground, the deer is not being shot in the water . . . or so the hunters say. It sounds like a gray area to me, and although legal, it smacks of taking unfair advantage of a fine game animal.

These ten ambush sites are some of the finest areas in which to knock down a nice buck. With a little original thinking all can be adapted for use during bow season. Some require preseason scouting; all demand a hunting position downwind from where deer should appear; and others demand the use of other equipment. But nothing offers the magical excitement of ambushing a buck on his own terrain except possibly stalking him.

And that, my friends, is the next chapter.

CHAPTER 6

Stalking the Fringeland Deer

Whitetail deer in fringe areas are reasonably easy to stalk. Note I said "reasonably"; nowhere are they a leadpipe cinch. They are cautious, spooky and fearful of humans.

You can stalk a whitetail successfully if you select suitable terrain, spot him before he sees you, use the wind to your advantage, and let natural noises cover any noise you make.

Stalks can be one- or two-man affairs, and of the two I prefer the two-man stalk only because one hunter stays behind and signals to the moving hunters when the going is clear. A one-man stalk offers as much enjoyment as a medium-rare steak and a solid sundowner after a long day afield, but it is more difficult to bring to fruition than stalking with a partner.

My twin brother George and I teamed up one time to stalk a nice buck, and it worked. We've tried it on other occasions, and have met with good and bad luck. One thing about stalking fringeland whitetails: It's never easy, but the suspense is enough to keep the adrenalin flowing for days.

It was late November, and the morning sun rose cold and yellow in the eastern sky, and the last soft snowflakes drifted lazily down to form an inch of fresh powder on the ground. The conditions were perfect for a late-season stalk on a whitetail buck I'd been watching for days. I rolled along smoothly toward George's house and glassed open fields for sign of the buck. My eyes scoped brushy draws and sidehills for sign of the animal. The buck had a distinctive track, and apparently an old wound caused him to drag his left hind leg.

Several deer crossed the side road on the way to George's house, and I checked each track. A few were does with young-of-the-year fawns, and one may have been a buck traveling alone, but he didn't wear the proper footgear and didn't walk with a pronounced limp. We wanted that gimpy-footed buck because I felt he may have trouble making it through the winter. His rack was not great, but his injury made him crafty.

I cut a smoking-hot track near the section where George lived. Previous sightings of the animal caused me to suspect the buck bedded down in a small swale near an adjacent swamp. I examined the track and learned that it was Ol' Gimp-along. The buck's track looked like he was cutting corners and would cross George's road on the way to his secluded bedding area. It was a hunch on my part, but I felt I was close to the animal at that time.

I slowed my pickup truck briefly and watched as the gimpy buck cut across the road 100 yards away. I was convinced this ol' boy would be hanging on our buckpole long before the day was out. We were confident we knew where he would hole up, and it was just a matter of our making all the right moves. Our knowledge of the terrain and the buck's habits gave us all we needed to pull off a classic stalk.

"This is going to be too easy," I thought to myself as the truck wheeled into George's driveway one-quarter mile from where the buck crossed the road. It had all the makings of a quick and easy stalk, and since he hadn't filled his tag the buck would be his if we scored.

I told George of spotting the buck's tracks and second-guessing where he would cross, and where I thought he would bed down. We drank hot coffee. George stuffed four .44 Magnum hollowpoints into his Ruger, grabbed his Bushnell 8 × 40 binoculars, donned a blaze-orange vest and we were off.

I pulled my binoculars from the truck, and we eased down the side road to where the buck had crossed. My travel down the road had not bothered the animal. Since the earlier heavy hunting pressure had dwindled to nothing, evidently this guy wasn't too worried about hunters. I saw the buck dawdle 100 yards into the field from the road. He walked 50 yards one direction and doubled back. Then he headed towards a hill behind George's barn.

"He's looking for a spot to bed down," George said, as we took up the track. The wind was in our face, and we knew once the buck bedded down it would be in a location where he could smell an enemy upwind and still watch his backtrack.

The tracks led over the hill. My brother recalled seeing other bucks bed down in a tiny swale behind the barn, and he wanted to check it out. It doesn't pay to ignore any cover.

"I'll belly up to the crest of the hill and check the swale with my binoculars," he said. "We don't want to go bopping in on the buck, and spook him into the next county."

He bellied down in the snow and squirmed up to the crest. With his binoculars he studied the swale 50 yards away for several minutes before sliding back down to my position.

"The tracks went into the swale," he said. "They also went out the other side. From my vantage point I could see the entire swale, and the deer wasn't there. I glassed each stump pile and overturned log, and finally spotted his track heading out. He's still moving."

We bellied up to the crest of the hill and glassed a standing cornfield 100 yards away.

A moving buck, once the rut has passed, often will gobble down a last-minute snack before packing it in for the day. The standing corn was sparse and in a small field, and had the buck been in the corn we could have seen him. This deer apparently wasn't hungry. Finally we picked up his tracks heading through the corn and into a brushy fencerow.

Fringeland bucks often bed where they can watch their backtrail and where prevailing breezes will carry the scent of approaching danger to them. Favorite bedding locations are in slashings, berry patches in thick woodlots, drainage ditches, small swales and other heavy cover. They occasionally bed on a small knob of brushy land slightly higher than the surrounding countryside, a position that gives them an advantage over predators.

We hunkered over, and one by one crossed the field to the far edge of the corn. The tracks were strung out in a neat, dark line against the new snow and they headed right for the fencerow. So far, so good.

We followed the general direction of the tracks to the fencerow with our binoculars, and couldn't be certain which way the buck went once he reached the fence. He could have turned north toward a sumac thicket 100 yards away, turned south toward a brushy swale or jumped the fencerow and continued straight across another open field toward a nearby swamp.

"Which way do you think he went?" George whispered. "Do you think he'll bed down in the sumac?"

"I've never seen a buck or a doe use that sumac clump," I said. "It's too exposed, and it's too close to that fencerow. If I were a buck I'd be inclined to jump the fence or go south toward the swale.

"Let's sneak over to the fencerow and find out. We'll take it one step at a time. Watch me for hand signals. If I see the buck I'll motion for you to stay down. We don't want to blow the stalk now, and really we're only thirty minutes behind the deer."

We crossed to the fencerow and began circling to sort out the buck's track. The animal had moved north along the fence, turned around and headed south, and then doubled back to duck through a brushy gap in the overgrown fencerow. The tracks continued toward the swamp.

One thing that slows down a deer stalk on fresh snow is sorting out the tracks. In this case it wasn't too bad, but at other times it can be time consuming as the buck in question mixes with other deer.

More stalks are blown because a hunter barges right in on a buck without checking first to determine the animal's location. It's critical to spot the animal before it spots you, and this can only be done by proceeding with caution and checking the terrain from afar.

We kept a low rise of ground between us and the swamp 400 yards away, and worked into a position to check for sign up front. There we saw the buck's shake-a-leg tracks heading straight across the field toward the swamp. The open field turned into a weed field just before it entered the swamp. Such fields require diligent glassing. A buck can bed down in a tiny hollow in the weeds and become invisible unless he raises his head and the hunter spots sunlight glinting off antlers. A deer can bed down inside the weed field, along its edges or may continue on through. Only time-consuming glassing with binoculars will tell the story, and it's no time to press ahead without checking first.

We glassed the field for twenty minutes and picked it apart with our binoculars. No sign of the buck.

"Let's circle the field as much as possible. We'll cover the downwind and cross-downwind sides first," I suggested. We checked the cross and downwind sides initially, and then slid downwind to look it over. The field was nearly bare outside the weed field, and we felt as exposed as two nudists at a baseball game.

I was wishing for my snow-white camouflage clothing, and was about to mention to George that the buck had to be inside the weed field, when we spotted his track heading back away from the swamp and over a small hill. The tiny ridge barely concealed a tiny ice-covered ditch and another adjoining weed field.

Our spirits lifted because we knew the buck was still ahead of us, and he didn't have a clue we were on his trail. His tracks were unhurried, and by now had nearly sixty minutes headstart on us.

The deer led us through that field and wound in and out of another sumac swale without slowing down. We circled the last sumac clump, and suddenly a pheasant flushed 300 yards ahead of us. We thought it strange a wild bird would flush for no reason, and then considered the pheasant may have flushed ahead of the deer. We circled wide around the field, glassed it thoroughly and then intercepted the buck's tracks again.

We knew the deer was still traveling ahead of us, and was slanting slightly away. We also knew we were close, and would have to be extremely careful to avoid closing with the animal. We realized we would have to move slow and take no chances in order to keep the buck from spotting our movements or getting our scent.

"There are some fallen trees along the edge of the upcoming woods," George said, pointing ahead. "The buck may be there or he may continue through the woods and lay up next to the lake."

We swiftly followed the dragging footprints through the new snow and stopped just below the crest of a small rise. We glassed the next weed field while standing near a towering oak but couldn't see the deer. We were just getting ready to move out along the tracks when I happened to catch the sight of sunlight glinting off antlers in a tiny fencerow near the downed trees. I couldn't be sure, but it looked like a deer's body with its antlers silhouetted against the morning sun.

"Hold it," I said, "I think I see his antlers."

I focused my 7 X 35 binoculars on the animal, and found myself looking at the buck's twitching ear and his polished antlers. The rack wasn't terribly big, but if we could pull off this stalk it would be a good buck for anyone.

The buck's tail was switching back and forth, and his head was swiveled around so he could watch his backtrail. The shot was far too long for George's .44 Magnum. If we had topped out over the hill instead of stopping just below the crest the buck would have seen us and been long gone.

"There he is," I told George. "He looks like he's bedded down in that tiny fencerow leading down to the woodlot near the fallen trees. If he stays there we'll have good cover most of the way for a stalk."

My brother scampered up the hill, cautiously eased his head over the crest and quickly picked out the buck in the fencerow. "What a spot," he said. "Hey, wait a minute. He just lay down in the thick brush, and appears to be looking the other way."

I took a look and confirmed George's suspicions. The buck was facing away from us, a lucky break. We'd have to move while his head was turned from us. Fortunately, the wind was still in our face.

We quickly worked out a set of hand signals, and took just enough time to double-check the buck again. We timed his movements, and once a minute he would leisurely turn around and check his backtrail.

"We'll move out, one by one, as soon as his head turns," George said. "I'll go first, and once I've crossed this open field you head out the next time he turns away."

Our signals were simple. If the spotter held up one hand it meant the other hunter should stop—immediately. If the spotter gave a go-ahead he would move out fast, run low to the ground and keep his progress as silent as possible.

The buck's head swiveled around as he studied his backtrail for a moment, and then turned his nose into the wind. George moved out first and crossed the open weed field. Our first goal was to gain the concealment of the fallen trees without being spotted, and this would place us within 100 yards of the buck.

George made it with little problem, and then it was my turn. I had to freeze twice while crossing the open field as the buck lifted his antlered noggin for a look around. Each time George caught the motion of the buck lifting his head, and since I wasn't watching the deer but was watching him I caught the hands-up motion and stopped moving. Both times the buck looked the other way, and then settled back for another minute of relaxation.

I crossed the finish line, fell in beside George near a jumble of wind-tossed trees and breathed a sigh of relief. We were close now, but George had discovered an obstacle we hadn't couned on—an old farmer's fence.

"What are we going to do about the fence?" I whispered.

"Beats hell out of me," he said. "Let's get to the fence first without being spotted and we'll figure something out. We're within 100 yards, and it looks we'll have to be within 50 yards before I can get a clean shot at the buck."

We bellied down along the fence and began moving out like infantrymen under fire. Head and butt down, we progressed for 25 yards without being spotted. It was slow going as we looked for a break in the old fence. We didn't want squeaking wires to give us away at this stage of the game.

We covered another 10 yards when a solitary crow flew over. Its loud caws sounded like a death knell on our stalk, and we froze in place as the buck lifted his head and stared our way. The deer looked up at the crow, back to the ground near our concealed position, and then went back to checking the wind. Fortunately the crow continued on its way. I saw George breathe a sigh of relief.

We quickly took turns closing the distance to the fence's junction with another fence. This would prove to be the turning point in our buck stalk, and either we got George on the other side of the fence or we gave up.

The early morning sun was up even with the treetops, and less than a quarter mile away we could hear the muffled jabber of kids waiting for the school bus. A thought came to my mind: The buck probably bedded down in the area each day and was accustomed to hearing the school bus clatter down George's bumpy road. The plan was simple. We'd time George's progress over, through or under the fence with the noise of the bus. It was crazy enough to work, and any sounds he made may be covered up by the kids or the bus as it bounced along the washboard road.

We talked the plan over, and George thought it might work.

"It sounds a tad far-fetched to me, but it's just crazy enough to work," he whispered. "But we'd better find a crossing spot in this fence within the next few minutes or we'll miss our chance."

George slipped off down the fenceline while I watched the buck. It continued to study its backtrail once each minute, and seemed to spend the rest of the time checking the wind and studying the terrain ahead of the brushy fencerow. He waved me down the fenceline, and within a minute I pulled up alongside him. He put his lips to my ear and whispered, "We're in luck. Here's a spot where I can crawl under the fence. I hope I can make it through when the bus comes along."

No sooner were the words out than we could hear the rumble and clatter of the school bus battering its way down the bumpy road. We looked at the buck, now only 60 yards away but still concealed by the brushy fencerow, its attention riveted on the sound of the bus. We were nearly broadside to the buck at this point, and since it was listening to the approaching bus George prepared to go under the fence. "Try not to make it squeak," I warned. "That buck is antsy enough right now, and although he's listening to the bus a squeak from this direction may ruin everything."

He took one more look at the buck, nodded his head in agreement and wiggled under the fence like a rattler burrowing under a warm rock. The fence didn't squeak. I elected to stay where I was while George bellied down in thin weeds and made his way to an old piece of rusting farm machinery barely 20 yards from the buck. He made it while the buck continued to stare at the sound of the school bus.

The buck's head was nearly invisible from my vantage point, but his snow-white antlers stood out in marked relief from the brushy fencerow. He apparently had listened to the school bus daily, and seemed curious about the sounds. The bus stopped, kids piled aboard and the bus clattered off down the road.

The deer turned his head around and wind-checked the surroundings. He shot a quick glance at his backtrail, and as he did George shuffled sideways along the farm machinery and into position for a shot. George kneeled next to the rusting equipment, slowly raised his .44 Magnum and savored the moment. This, the end of a stalk, is the epitome of excitement; the kill is anticlimactic. I knew George had the buck dead to rights, and I knew he'd take the shot as the buck turned to study his backtrail. But now he wanted to enjoy the moment.

The seconds seemed to pass on tired feet. Nearly a minute passed, and then the buck turned his head slowly to check the trail he'd made walking in to his bedding area.

George slowly raised his rifle, centered the iron sights on the buck's neck and squeezed the trigger. The buck lurched once and rolled over.

To be truthful, not all stalks end like this one. Many are spoiled when a buck spots a moving hunter, or when too much noise or an errant breeze carries scent to the animal.

Stalking fringeland deer is moderately difficult, but not impossible. Let's take a look at the ingredients that go into a successful stalk, and what hunters can do to tip the scales in their favor. The ingredients in this deer-stalking stew include knowing the wind, knowing the terrain, spotting the buck before he spots you, using nearby every-day noises to cover your sounds; also, deer nervousness and curiosity.

Knowing the Wind

Whitetails are scent conscious and use the wind when traveling from feeding to bedding areas and back. Stalking deer hunters must play the wind like a fine violin and keep it in their face most of the time. There are any number of ways to check wind direction. Bowhunters often tie a pom-pom or string to their bow to check the wind, and gun hunters can do the same. I smoke, and use cigarette smoke to gauge wind direction and intensity. A bottle of unscented Puff powder is good; a single squirt of the powder can reveal wind direction in an instant. Many hunters check the wind when a stalk first begins, and never check it again during the hunt. Checking your rifle for proper cartridges or checking to see if the safety is on contribute to a safe hunt, but checking the wind often is the key to a successful stalk on fringeland deer.

Form the habit of checking the wind each time you stop to glass ahead for a buck. This habit is critical once you've closed to within 100 yards of an animal, and it is every bit as crucial to success as watching the bedding buck when each movement is made.

Stalks can be made crosswind providing the hunter stays on the cross-downwind side of the deer. A stalk cross-upwind is as destined for failure as a stalk from directly upwind. Only a foolhardy hunter would try to stalk a bedded buck when scent is being carried downwind to the deer. Bucks almost always bed down where they can view their backtrail and where they can check the prevailing breeze. Calm days are best for a stalk, although I've had limited success on extremely windy days when the breeze is steady from one quarter. Never stalk deer when the wind switches from one quarter to another.

Puff wind-direction powder is good for checking errant breezes.

Know Your Terrain

A firm knowledge of local terrain is very important when stalking fringeland deer. It does little good to know a buck has roosted in a specific location only to learn it is impossible to stalk close enough for a shot.

Chapter 2 of this book discussed learning the terrain. A solid knowledge of the countryside where you hunt is especially important when stalking deer. Study terrain spring, summer and fall, and learn what it looks like when snow covers the ground if you live in northern climes.

Know where fencerows lead and where they originate; learn the locations of tiny swales, swamps or clumps of brush; know the configuration of swamps or cattail marshes; learn how rolling hills and brushy woodlots tie in with other terrain features—in other words, learn your hunting area well and study it as often as possible until all features are indelibly imprinted on your mind.

Learn to anticipate how a moving buck will follow terrain features. Bucks often fall into one of two categories—open field travelers or heavy cover movers. If a buck crosses a road through a wooded area he probably always moves through heavy cover. If the buck, like the one recounted at the beginning of this chapter, crosses an open field he'll

This buck was bedded down in a low-lying swale bordered by sumac.

probably stick to open areas all the way to his bedding site. Whitetail bucks are creatures of habit, and like humans they resist changes.

I once blew a stalk on a nice eight-point buck because I didn't have a firm knowledge of the terrain. It taught me a valuable lesson.

A buck had crossed a road during the night along a dry brushy creekbed and continued along the ditch through heavy cover. "Aha," I thought, reading sign in the fresh snow, "a brush traveler." This was years ago, and I figured I was as savvy as Dan Boone when it came to unraveling buck tracks. What I hadn't learned was that bucks know where they will bed, and it's usually where they can see or smell approaching danger.

I didn't know the terrain, and thirty minutes into the stalk I topped a rise in plain view of the world. Fifty yards away a low-lying swale bordered by sumac and brush stood out like a wart on my nose. The buck was facing into the wind, and was watching his backtrail like a bad guy casing his next bank to rob.

As I topped the rise the buck slammed out of that swale like a Saturn rocket leaving the launching pad. He took three steps, and placed a wall of brush and a small hill between us before I could raise the rifle to my shoulder.

I had blundered into that buck, and like a teenager on a big date with the prettiest gal in town, I felt as conspicuous as if I'd just dumped a bowl of soup in my lap. The buck was gone, and I felt dejected. I had ankled into the area without knowing the terrain, and it had cost me a shot at a nice buck. Had I known the countryside I would have realized a swale lay just over the hill, and would have circled around on its downwind side and checked everything out. Instead, I boosted that buck into a blind, panicky flight and failed to get a shot.

This is, however, the manner in which lessons are learned.

Don't just learn the terrain, but really study it like a geography lesson in high school. Know where deer travel, and where they bed down or feed. Learn terrain lessons well, and you'll be on the right track when the time comes to stalk a fringeland buck in open or brushy country.

Spot the Buck First

This lesson in stalking fringeland bucks is so elementary many will wonder why it is mentioned. Unfortunately, I know many hunters who have blown a stalk within the first few minutes by being spotted by the whitetail. Learn to locate the deer before it spots you.

Good binoculars are indispensable when stalking deer. A quality spotting scope is an asset, but is clumsy and cumbersome to use when moving along on a trail of fresh deer tracks. The trick to spotting and stalking a buck before he sees you is to bring those binoculars into play often. Mountain hunters have long known the secret of plunking your fanny down and glassing faraway slopes. The fringeland deer hunter should take a tip from mountain hunters and learn to use binoculars to check terrain.

Ease up to the crest of a hill, and slowly inch your head over. Use nearby cover to break up your silhouette. Glass tracks in sand or snow, and check as far ahead as possible for sign of the buck. Do not, as I did, stumble over a hill thinking the buck may be a long distance away. He can be, and often is, very close.

Bring your knowledge of terrain and wind direction into play. Ask yourself: "Where would I bed down so I can sniff the wind and still be able to watch my backtrail?"

The author (left) glasses ahead with a Bushnell spotting scope. Below, a hunter uses binoculars to scout the terrain for deer.

Opposite: Learn to spot the buck before it sees you. This animal was nearly invisible except when it turned its head and flicked its ears.

Answer this question, and you'll be a leg-up on other deer stalkers. Learn to anticipate deer movements, and learn to use binoculars to study the terrain.

Binocular use is a studied art. Learn to pick the terrain apart, and to look for horizontal shadows or lines in an otherwise vertical landscape. Become accustomed to taking a field, woods, fencerow or weed field apart inch by inch, and look not for a whole animal but for the glint of sunlight on antlers or the flick of an ear or tail. Never look for a whole deer, but instead look for movement or something that appears out of place in the surrounding environment.

Even when a buck beds down he is in motion. Ears flick, the tail moves, the body moves and the head may turn. A brief glimpse of movement may reveal an unseen buck bedded down in an area you just glassed. Never hurry a glassing job, but instead use patience. Double- and triple-check an area before committing yourself to a move through it.

Learn to glass ahead, and to do so from cover. Never commit yourself to a move unless you are 100 percent sure the animal is not present, and then never take a whitetail buck for granted. I've seen bucks move through an area and then double back in a moment of indecision. Remember, bucks and all whitetail deer are spooky and often will do the unexpected. That's what keeps some bucks alive from one season to another.

Whitetail Nervousness

This book has stressed the fact that whitetail deer are a spooky lot. They are frightened of their own shadow, unknown noises, hints of danger from unknown sources and have been known to flee when a bluejay or crow flies overhead. It takes very little to frighten deer. If a hunter bears this in mind he can pull off a succesful stalk.

Simply remember that whitetails are cautious and smart. Always be cognizant of the fact that a buck (or doe) will spook at any noise it can't immediately identify, and will probably run for several hundred yards if frightened by a strange movement.

Whitetail nervousness should be foremost in a hunter's mind when he begins a stalk. Look for the animal to lay up in unexpected locations, and realize that deer are on pins and needles throughout the bedding period. Never take the animal for granted, but instead learn to anticipate this nervousness and use it to your advantage throughout the stalk.

Whitetail Curiosity

I've watched whitetails spot hunter movement in a haybale blind, and have been amazed several times to see the deer take cautious, inching steps forward in an effort to determine just what had caught their attention. Other times, I've seen whitetail bucks curious about the sounds of passing vehicles or children's voices.

I once shot a nice buck along Michigan's busy interstate—I-94. The buck had bedded down in thick cover near the interstate's fenceline, and it was intently watching the cars and trucks whizzing past on the freeway.

I had stalked the buck for a quarter-mile, and I knew whitetails often bed down near the fence. A big eighteen-wheeler came burping down the road with loud backfires and a faulty engine. The buck seemed fascinated by the strange sounds, and didn't hear my final approach. In fact the last thing he heard was my shotgun coughing up a lethal dose of one-ounce 12-gauge slugs. One heavy slug caught the buck in the neck, the other behind the shoulder, and he died probably thinking the loud noises were backfires from the truck.

Curiosity is only aroused in whitetails which are not overly spooked by heavy hunting pressure. If the animal feels safe, and has no reason to suspect human intrusion into the area, deer may become curious about strange noises or movements. But don't think for a moment that deer won't bolt once they satisfy themselves that the movement or noise may constitute a danger to them.

Look for curiosity when stalking deer, but don't count on it in all cases. Whitetails are far spookier than they are curious.

Use Everyday Noises

A whitetail deer, in a reasonably relaxed state (when the animal is bedded down and feels somewhat secure), tends to view everyday noises with mixed feelings. The sounds of a squirrel scurrying through pin oaks is common, and the cawing of a crow a quarter-mile away is another example of everyday sounds deer are used to hearing.

However, a squirrel scolding a stalking hunter 50 yards away is enough to put a whitetail buck on Red Alert. A crow that spots hunter movement and circles overhead as he calls to his black buddies for reinforcements offers another threat to the buck's well-being. A frightened bluejay once spooked a buck for me when I was within 50 yards of the animal, and the last I saw of the deer was his white flag disappearing into a swamp.

Learn to use everyday noises heard by whitetails to your advantage. School buses travel on regular schedules, and homeowners leave for work at certain times, and these sounds are commonplace for fringeland bucks. Use them often when hunting.

The clatter of a school bus can cover the sound of a squeaking fence, and the rustle of a squirrel digging nuts can be used to mask the sound of a hunter traveling through heavy weeds. As long as a sound is not foreign it will not spook deer providing it doesn't come from an unexpected direction. Be prepared to listen for and identify natural sounds, and be ready to incorporate their use into your stalk.

CHAPTER 7

Deer Drives
That Work

The cold November wind was blowing tiny BB-sized chunks of sleet into my face as I leaned against a tall oak and strained my eyes for the first sign of an approaching deer. My hunting buddy and I had been on stand for thirty minutes as the two drivers circled upwind around the 10-acre woodlot before beginning their downwind mini-drive.

Suddenly a buck materialized through the storm like a wraith from a horror movie, and began mincing downwind toward me along the woodlot's edge. He would stop for ten or fifteen seconds and stand motionless, looking around. Twice he stared my way only to swivel his head around to study the sounds of drivers zigzagging toward him.

This buck wasn't a grizzled old veteran of the deer wars, but he was cagey and wasn't fond of being pressured into moving in this direction. He was being crowded, and he knew it. The buck didn't have anywhere to go except downwind, and if I remained motionless the animal would soon be in my lap.

The buck was partially screened by heavy berry bushes and brush, and when he moved it reminded me of an Indian fakir walking on broken glass. Each step was studied deliberation. Within seconds the deer disappeared from sight between two large oak trees.

I used the opportunity to shoulder my Remington 12-gauge pump shotgun and get ready. I knew the buck would soon be within range. He appeared again from behind a thin screening of trees and brush, and studied the terrain ahead. He wasn't taking any chances, but being upwind of me he had no way of knowing I'd set up camp in his backyard.

The buck apparently satisfied himself about an absence of danger, and turned my way. As he bounded across a clearing 10 yards in front of me, I held on his shoulder and touched off the shot. The 3-inch magnum load of 41 No. 4 buckshot caught him in the shoulder, chest and neck, and he covered only 15 yards before toppling.

That five-point buck was the third buck our four-man party of hunters had taken in two days using a system we call the mini-drive. One buck was a massive nine-pointer with heavy beams and long, thick points. The other buck was a large trophy eleven-pointer, and we had become accustomed to seeing bucks nearly every day with this hunting system.

Driving deer is an oldtime hunting philosophy with roots buried in antiquity, and it can be a productive way to hunt fringeland deer. Unfortunately, the driving techniques used by many hunters leave too many holes for deer to escape. The trick is to turn those holes into dead-end alleys.

A knowledge of deer movements and terrain features is of paramount importance to the success of a deer drive. It does little good to push deer in the desired direction unless the animal knows he has easy access to heavy cover along the route.

Most deer drives fail because hunters attack a cover with a shotgun approach. They make too much noise, advertise their presence and hit the cover from first one angle and then another. A drive should be orchestrated, and one man with intimate knowledge of the area must be the conductor. His job is to place drivers and standers where they will be most effective.

I hunt whitetails each fall with Roger Kerby of Buckley, Michigan, who happens to be one of the best deer drivers I've met. Each year our success with whitetail bucks averages about 80 to 85 percent, and in a state like Michigan where the statewide hunter success ratio is about 18 percent, our score is indeed high. Many of Kerby's tactics will be explained later.

Strict attention must be paid to details. Little things often overlooked can offer avenues of escape to a driven buck. Errors in judgment seldom produce bucks on deer drives.

Another important point to remember when driving fringeland deer is to concentrate your efforts on small covers. We've all seen the massive deer drives where literally dozens of hunters stand around jabbering like monkeys picking fleas while they try to hammer out a decision on how a particular piece of hunting turf will be driven. Chances are good the conversation will take place within hearing distance of the cover, and then everyone splits up into groups of standers and drivers. More chatter, more noise. Is it any wonder that a self-respecting buck will have used the confusion to vamoose?

"Hey Joe, you get over by that dead elm and stand still," one hunter will say.

"Which dead elm?"

"That big one by the swamp, dummy."

The words are yelled back and forth, and finally Joe sashays off in the general direction of an elm tree to watch the swamp's edge. Meanwhile, up and down the line a herd of vocal hunters is aligning themselves near the cover to be driven in hopes a buck will come to them and offer something other than a fleeting shot. In the meantime the drivers are going through similar noisy movements at the other end of cover. They ready their pots, pans, whistles and other noisemakers, and the drive begins.

Everyone, according to deer-driving legend, must walk side by side. In practice, the stronger-walking driver will forge ahead of his buddies while they stumble through the woods, and within minutes a hole exists large enough to drive a battalion of Sherman tanks through.

Any guesses where remaining whitetails will head? They will lie low as the noisy drivers filter by, and then calmly get up and escape through the hole. The drivers, intent on making an unholy din which they believe will move deer ahead of them, seldom see deer as they are too engrossed in trying to keep the line tight and to make more noise.

Bah!

I participated in only one such drive and thought putting up storm windows would be more fun.

Such a drive has several strikes against it before it begins. It often takes place in a large area where hunters lose track of each other and the direction they should be traveling. Other problems include too much noise and limited knowledge of terrain.

Maintains deer guide Roger Kerby, "The secret of success when driving deer is to make silent drives downwind after standers have silently moved into position. We choose small parcels of cover for our drives, and we comb them in a systematic manner. We make no noise, never talk and we push deer in the direction they want to go. We don't try to drive deer upwind, and we don't try to push deer in such a way they resort to blind, panicked flight. We want to keep 'em moving slowly ahead of us. This offers standers good shots at slow-moving animals."

Kerby serves as the drive master. It's a one-man job, and although he confers with me or his guide Lee Blahnik it's clear who is in charge. Roger is the main man because he knows the terrain, knows where bucks usually bed down in the cover to be driven, and knows where the animals will head when a slow-moving driver approaches. He knows the best ambush spots for standers, and he's as ugly as a grizzly bear with a toothache if someone messes up. His knowledge of the terrain he hunts is incredible. Invariably he will choose an isolated bit of cover generally passed over by other hunters, and it's in these areas we score on hefty whitetail bucks.

The game plan is the same, cover after cover. We'll gather at our hunting vehicles one-half mile or more from the area to be driven and quietly make our plans.

"OK gang, we're going to drive the sidehill," Kerby announces.

A small cheer goes up from those of us who have been in on buck kills on the sidehill.

"Dave," Kerby says, pointing to me, "you know where the bucks come out. You take two standers, and put one at the top of the sidehill where it pinches down and the other where the little gulley comes up out of the hill. No talking from now on, hear?"

I nod in agreement because I know I'll be sitting on top of a little knob overlooking a field, and any conversation once we near the sidehill can spook wary bucks. My presence serves as a stopgap in case a buck slicks out past one of the other standers and tries to gain his freedom across the open field.

We move silently into position. I'll station the other hunters, and if they've never

Roger Kerby, deer guide and drivemaster (camo hat), softly explains the upcoming drive to the hunters. Even though they are a half-mile from the hunting area, he forbids loud talking.

hunted the area I'll lead them by the hand to the proper location. They are cautioned not to move until we come for them, and I point out where the buck will generally appear. All this is done in sign language without uttering a word. Then I'll ease out of the area and climb my hill. Then it becomes a waiting game.

The covers we drive are chosen with care. Each offers known escape routes for bucks, and each is longer than it is wide. Many covers may be 100 to 300 yards in length, but measure no more than 100 yards in width. Some spots we drive are only 30 to 50 yards wide.

One sidehill we drive is some 300 yards in length, but is less than 50 yards wide at its widest point. The cover is thick, and this is why few hunters venture inside. It offers superb bedding cover for whitetails, and two or three good escape routes at the downwind end. It's along these routes that bucks head when the pressure gets heavy, but we always have someone there to greet them.

Kerby and Blahnik generally drive the sidehill. Actually, one man can do it as well as two providing he moves back and forth from one side of the cover to the other. The drivers stop and start, but remain within eye contact of each other. They make no noise, and on more than one occasion Kerby has shot a buck in his bed while the deer watches Blahnik passing nearby. It frequently takes them one hour to circle around to the upwind end and begin the drive. This gives standers plenty of time to get into position and get comfortable before the drive begins.

The standers are positioned in such locations that they can see approaching deer and spot the drivers coming along behind. The only danger in driving deer occurs when a stander shoots at an approaching buck without thinking of the drivers behind the animal. Kerby stations standers where they can look down on the action, and spot the deer and drivers at the same time. In eight years of driving deer we've never had an accident or a near miss.

"I try to work the cover so slowly that bucks slowly ooze out in front of the standers," Kerby states. "Push them too fast and too hard, and they will squirt out the sides in panicked flight and no one gets a decent shot."

Mind you, not all deer drives work. If they did, everyone would adopt this hunting strategy. But drives will work providing each piece of cover is hazed in the proper manner.

Our success rate is about one buck for each three or four driven covers. We've had times when we would take two, sometimes three, bucks from one cover. We've also had times when we've driven eight or ten covers in one day and never saw a buck.

That's deer hunting.

Driving deer is a hunting method compatible with much of North America's fringeland areas. Fringeland whitetail habitat usually is a series of heavy cover pockets surrounded by open fields or croplands. It's a mix of heavy and sparse cover, creekbeds, drainage ditches, clumps of swamp or marsh and the like. It's in these tiny pockets of heavy cover where bucks hole up during hunting season, and it's here deer drives can find action providing they go about it in the correct manner.

Let's take a brief look at the elements needed to drive deer, and the various types of covers likely to be encountered.

Pick Small Covers

Small covers mean just that. Choose a cover long and narrow, and with brushy terrain inside. The downwind end should be the narrowest.

Cover to be driven should be no more than 150 yards wide; 75 to 100 yards wide is ideal. Forget about wide, extremely long covers and instead pick something from 100 to 300 yards in length.

Choose covers that other hunters ignore for one reason or another. Many of our favorite covers are filled with dense cedars, tag alders and/or swamp where it is tough for drivers to move in an upright position. Some spots are driven on hands and knees as it is impossible to walk. Find a spot where you stumble over and around deadfalls, and spend more time climbing over and under thick cover, and you'll have found an ideal spot to drive providing it meets the length and width requirements.

The Sounds of Silence

Leave your police whistles, pots and pans at home. Move drivers into position on the upwind side without noise. Standers must be in position long before the drivers start moving through the cover. Standers must move into position as noiselessly as possible, and this means absolutely no talking for the last quarter-mile.

Do not drive vehicles up to the hunting area, and even if cars and trucks are parked a half-mile away do not slam car doors. Ease them shut quietly, and make no more noise than is necessary to load firearms and to walk to the hunting area.

Refrain from stepping on dry twigs as you enter the area where you will stand. Silently brush all dried leaves from underfoot, and clear debris away so you can pivot silently for a shot at a passing buck. Then, learn to sit or stand still. Do not move or make any noise.

Choose Firearms Carefully

We choose our firearms with care. Where we will stand dictates our choice of gun. If we are driving we'll use a 12-gauge shotgun loaded with No. 4 buckshot or a Ruger .44 Magnum for close-range shots. If we plan to stand, and the cover is extremely thick, we'll often choose a shotgun loaded with buckshot or slugs. The key determining factor here is the distance from stander to where the deer will appear, and if it's inside of 30 yards we'll choose a buckshot-loaded 3-inch magnum 12-gauge every time.

If the cover is reasonably open, and the distance from stander to deer is from 30 to 100 yards, any rifle will serve the purpose providing the hunter is accustomed to the firearm. Standers who wait on hilltops or near fences overlooking wide-open spaces would do well to arm themselves with a flat-shooting rifle. A 4X scope helps hunters spot the animal, and to determine whether the deer carries antlers.

The foregoing are merely basics, and must be interpreted according to the terrain and the needs of hunters in each area. Judge for yourself what is needed, and adapt these policies which are not set in stone for use in each area.

The following drives work. Each will work best if practiced in similar areas as described. Each can be adapted somewhat to fit into local terrain features, but the orchestrated movements of drivers and standers must be closely adhered to if you wish to be successful. Do not be afraid to improvise, but do so in a cautious manner after once learning how each technique is supposed to work.

The Mini-Drive

The mini-drive is one of my favorites, so named because it can be used by three or four hunters working as a team. Terrain must be chosen carefully if only three hunters are used, and depending on the size and shape of the cover either one or two men can serve as drivers or one or two hunters serve as standers with only one driver.

This drive is probably the most successful of all. It's very success, however, depends on a downwind movement of the driver(s) and silence of standers approaching their hunting station. It also depends on the hunters knowing the exact location of one or two escape routes or active deer trails leading to other heavy cover along the downwind side, and it means choosing a suitable ambush site nearby.

The hunters should approach the hunting area to be driven by walking upwind quietly. This approach will prevent deer from becoming aware of your presence until it is too late for them to leave the cover safely. A spoken word, snap of a twig or creak of a farmer's fence may spook a big buck from heavy cover long before you are within shooting range.

The standers must move into position without making a sound. Often a buck will lay up within 25 yards, and since mini-drives work best on long, narrow covers, any sounds made can easily be heard by a buck. Clear the stand of dead tree branches, dry leaves and twigs underfoot. Understand that standers may be in position for an hour, and this generally is the maximum amount of time needed to conduct a mini-drive. Many such drives have started and ended within fifteen minutes, and this is all the time that's needed to shoot a buck if everything goes well.

Choose a stand with nothing in front of you to impede the swing of rifle or shotgun. The stand site must be downwind of the escape route or active deer trail, and ideally it should be within 20 yards of where deer will appear.

The perfect stand will offer a tree or bush behind you to break up your outline.

Opposite: In the mini-drive, drivers walk upwind quietly. Standers move into position on downwind side thirty minutes before drivers circle around woodlot and begin the drive.

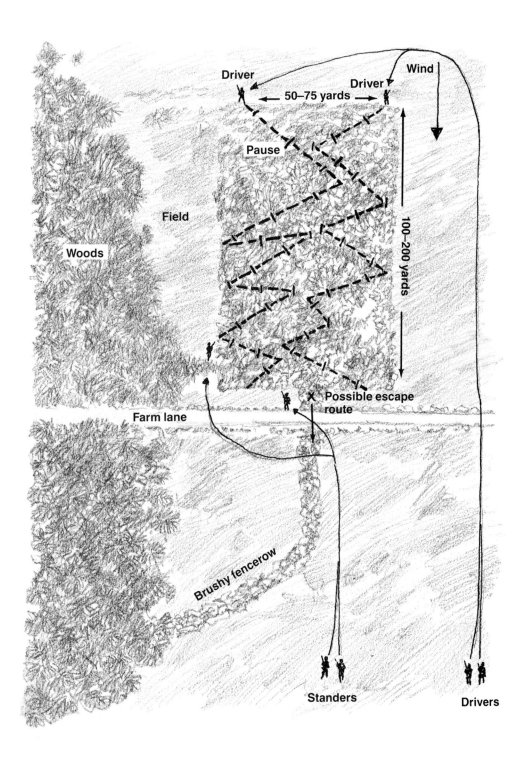

Kneel or sit to reduce your silhouette, and stand only when absolutely necessary. Standing hunters tend to move much more than a comfortable, sitting hunter.

The mini-drive works simply because the driver(s) scent drifts downwind toward the deer. The deer smells the slowly approaching hunters, and will move away from them. This means that a properly executed mini-drive will place a deer where you want him, and not where he necessarily wants to go.

This is based on the premise that deer—especially bucks—will move away from a

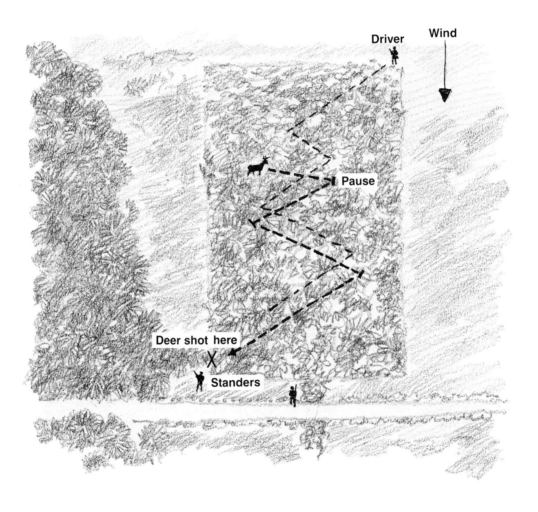

Bucks move away from a solitary driver. This knowledge can be used to haze bucks to the stander. Deer slide to the side opposite the driver, and are forced into exiting the woodlot where expected.

hunter while traveling downwind. If the hunter is on the left side of the cover the buck will almost always slide to the opposite—the right side—of the cover. If the hunter shifts his position to the right side the buck will cross to the left side. A group of hunters can use this knowledge, and the ability to shift from side to side at will, to be upwind of the deer and opposite the animal when they approach the end of the cover. This should place the buck directly in front of a waiting hunter.

Two drivers have a much better chance of hazing deer where they want him to go than does a single driver. Two drivers can synchronize their movements to cover the entire area, keeping each other in sight at all times while looking ahead for the buck.

The mini-drive must be executed slowly and quietly. Noise must be kept to a minimum, and should consist only of that made by two hunters moving downwind as silently as possible as they drift back and forth.

We've found the perfect drive means taking four or five steps, and then a stop for ten or fifteen seconds. A deer will often panic when we stop, and then bust out ahead of us and in front of waiting standers. After we take a brief pause we will take another few steps, stop again and look all around. It's quite similar to stillhunting.

A zigzag pattern of moving downwind prevents a buck from staying in one spot and letting a hunter walk past. If two hunters drive, one moves toward the other as he moves toward his edge of cover and then they move back toward the middle of the cover. This means, by starting and stopping and zigzagging, two hunters can cover a small area and prevent deer from circling around behind them. The best strategy is for one driver to be slightly ahead of the other.

One driver should start at the corner upwind and opposite the downwind stander. He moves from one side of the cover to the other, with sudden stops. He should move slowly, take a few steps and stop for a look-see. Once he reaches a point where he can clearly see the edge of the cover ahead, he should stop and move the opposite way at a 45-degree angle, stopping every few steps, until he reaches the edge. He then moves in stops and starts at a 45-degree angle toward the other side.

It's the frequent stops and starts, and changes of direction, that send whitetail bucks into a panic. Just time your direction changes so you'll be opposite the stander at the drive's end.

A trick we occasionally use is to carry a few small rocks. As we near thick brush during a drive we'll lob a rock or two ahead to spook out hiding deer. Sometimes it moves a hesitant deer.

We try to make small noises once we approach within gunshot range of standers. The caw-aww of a crow, or a bird whistle, will alert standers to your presence and it does not frighten deer. Use the call sparingly, and keep it low in volume. Move after each call, and do not allow a deer to pinpoint your position by such calls. A brief, low whistle serves the same purpose.

Some bucks are admittedly too smart to be fooled by a mini-drive. They will cross where least expected, leave the cover at the first hint of danger and can make a fool out of hunters.

Hillside Drives

This drive works very well in fringeland areas where hills are abundant and butt up against small lakes. I'm mindful of one location where Kerby and I hunt. We've taken a number of deer there through the years.

Picture it: a sidehill laced with cedars, pines and tamaracks, and only 50 yards from a tiny lake. The cover is thick and slightly wider at the upwind end than the downwind end. Bucks lay up here, and each year we take a number of them. The reason—they have nowhere to run.

Only two spots offer a buck any chance of escape. One is a small gully runnning up the sidehill, and the other is out through a 10-yard-wide natural funnel where the curving sidehill slides up next to the lake. A driven buck must head out one of the two locations, and we always have a hunter at each spot.

The driving technique used once standers are in position is similar to the mini-drive. The driver(s) move upwind and around to the upwind head of the sidehill, and then begin moving downwind in stops and starts. A lone driver will zigzag back and forth through the cover with frequent stops and starts, and two drivers will criss-cross back and forth, with frequent pauses, and to cover all available cover.

Usually the buck begins moving slowly downwind as the hunters approach. Downwind-drifting scent alerts the buck, and the slight noises made by the drivers moving through heavy cover compound the buck's panic problem. The result is he starts heading downwind while hoping to slip around behind the drivers.

Few bucks slip behind us because we choose narrow areas where visibility is reasonably good, and the buck is forced to keep moving downwind. Sooner or later he finds himself moving past one of the standing hunters, who makes the shot.

The trick is to locate an area where a sidehill butts up against a lake. The water prevents the buck from easy escape in that direction, and the sidehill serves as a funnel to move the animal where we want to go. The buck is caught in a box, and is forced to go where we choose. This method puts as much venison in our freezer as any driving method except the mini-drive. It really works!

The Dead-End Drive

This method of driving fringeland whitetails derives its name from the fact that our actions force deer into a dead-end. A buck caught in this drive runs into a brick wall at the end of an alley, and has nowhere to go . . . except where we want him to be.

All driving techniques listed in these pages are a variation of the mini-drive, and differ only in the locale in which they are used. The typical mini-drive may find deer squirting out the sides ahead of drivers and standers, but the dead-end drive will find bucks caught between the spoor and the stink.

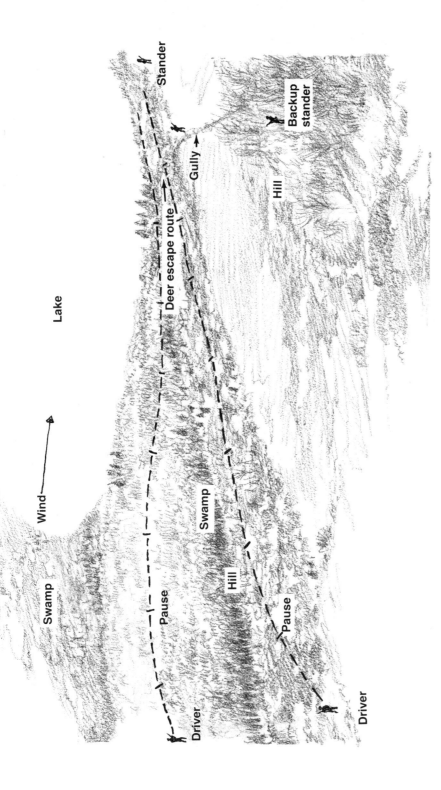

A sidehill laced with cedars, pines and tamaracks with a maximum distance of 50 yards from hill to lake. The sidehill narrows down and acts as a funnel for deer trying to escape the drivers. Standers are positioned at the narrow end, in a gully running up the sidehill and on a nearby hill.

We use dead-end drives for narrow fingers of swamp. The swamp may be dry with countless tag alders, or a wet and wild affair with standing water and countless cedars. Both areas produce bucks for us.

A dead-end drive necessitates locating prime cover with a road, lake or other natural barrier along one of the long sides. Everything must funnel down to a dead end, and a cover that ends at a highway or lake is the best. Whitetails caught in this type of drive must filter out one side, or find themselves facing oncoming traffic or deep water.

We'll station one man at the extreme end on the off chance a buck will try to cross a lake or road, but one or two standers will be positioned along the only side that offers an escape route. A gully, ravine, narrow finger of woods, fencerow or other cover along the open side will be where a buck will try to escape nine times out of ten, and if a hunter is properly positioned he'll get a shot. The man at the dead end serves only as a stop-gap measure, and seldom gets a shot.

Drivers work slowly downwind through the cover, and stop often for a brief look around. They zigzag, and often will spot a deer moving ahead as it tries to find a way out of the box. It goes without saying that a noiseless approach is important, and do not hurry when making the drive.

Standers should be in position at least thirty minutes before the drive starts, and snap shooting at rapidly moving targets is the rule. Once a buck knows that he is caught in a trap he'll try to make a move to get away, and this means stander sites must be chosen with care.

Flanker-Back Drive

We seldom use a flanker-back drive because much of the fringeland country we hunt, and the covers we choose for drives, are narrow enough that a flanker to cover our rear is not needed.

This drive is best suited to slightly larger covers where it's conceivable that a buck can sit tight and then slip back around a driver to escape to the rear. A flanker, properly positioned, will intercept the animal and get a shot.

The drive is set up like the mini-drive or dead-end drive, and although the drive is still made downwind a flanker covers the rear on two sides. The two drivers begin working downwind through the cover—one from each side—and once they are fifty yards into the cover one or two flankers slide in from the sides and cover the middle portions.

Opposite: A buck moves downwind ahead of the drifting scent of hunters-drivers and the slight noise they make during the drive.

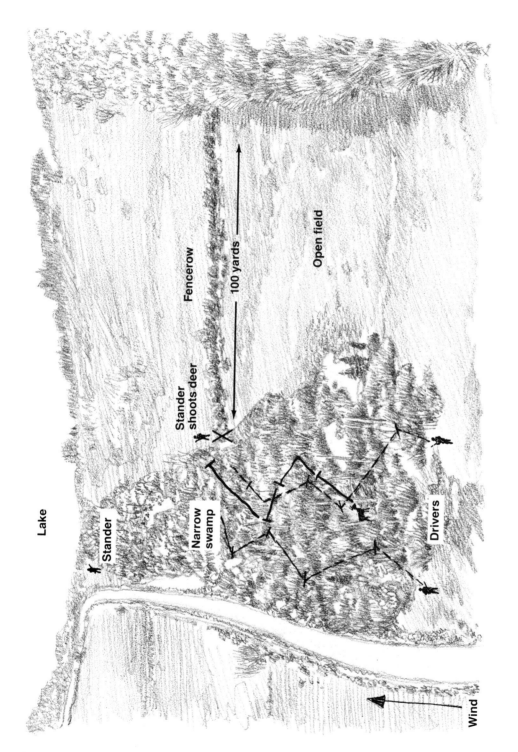

Lake

Stander

Narrow swamp

Drivers

Wind

Fencerow

Stander shoots deer

100 yards

Open field

A dead-end drive has a road or lake along one of the narrow sides. Deer usually try to escape along a thick fencerow into a nearby woods. One stander acts as a stopgap near the lake and road.

A deer which tries to circle behind the drivers will seldom travel the outside edges of the cover where it can be seen. Deer generally try to circle back into the middle of the cover and stay in the thicket.

The flankers move slowly, and stop often. They should use all available cover, and concentrate solely on that area between them and the drivers. They must look for the flicker of an ear or tail, a horizontal body line in a vertical environment, and be prepared to allow the deer to move past them before shooting to prevent an accident to the drivers.

Flankers must zigzag slightly but not as much as the drivers. They should stay at least 50 yards behind the drivers at all times, and move at a slower pace.

It's surprising, but in slightly larger covers a flanker-back drive often produces good deer. And, equally surprising, the flankers often do most of the shooting.

This happened to me one time. We were driving a narrow but extremely thick swamp, and I was the sole flanker. The drivers were moseying back and forth through the heavy cover, and I had just stopped for a quick look around. I caught a glimpse of a deer moving head-down through the swamp. It apparently had spotted the approaching drivers, laid down and once they passed had got up and began moving out of the swamp. The only problem was the deer was moving my way, and although I couldn't tell whether it was buck or doe its actions were suspiciously bucklike.

I froze like a granite statue, and the deer kept coming. It raised its head several times to look around, but the tag alders looked like antlers to me. It moved slowly past me only 20 yards away, and then it reached a tiny clearing and stood upright with head held high. It was a nice five-point buck.

I was carrying a wellworn .30/30 carbine that day. I dropped the front sights into the buckhorn back sight, nestled the front sight behind the buck's front shoulder and touched it off. The buck jumped as though scalded with boiling water, bolted into the tag alders and seconds later I heard him crash to earth.

The buck wasn't big by anyone's standards, but he was savvy enough to allow the drivers to pass him by. If I hadn't been following along and bringing up the rear that would have been one buck we never would have seen.

Flanker-back drives produce. Use them sparingly, and make sure the flanker moves slowly and stays far behind the main drivers.

The Stillhunt Drive

This deer-hunting method derives its name from the fact that hunters stillhunt and drive at the same time. It is best suited for large parcels of land which cannot be successfully driven without a small army of hunters. We execute this type of drive two or three times yearly, and it generally produces one or more bucks.

This technique can work in any area, although if a hunting location is too large,

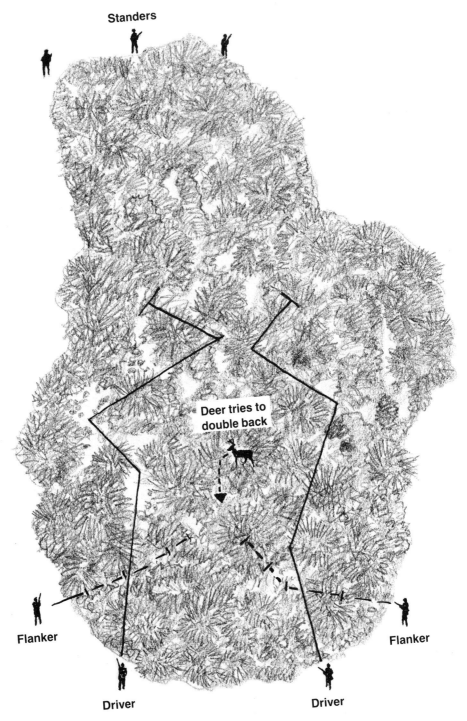

This drawing illustrates how a flanker-back drive should work. The drivers move downwind into the cover first, and once they are 50 yards inside the flankers slide in from the sides to cover the middle. Flankers stay at least 50 yards behind drivers and move slower.

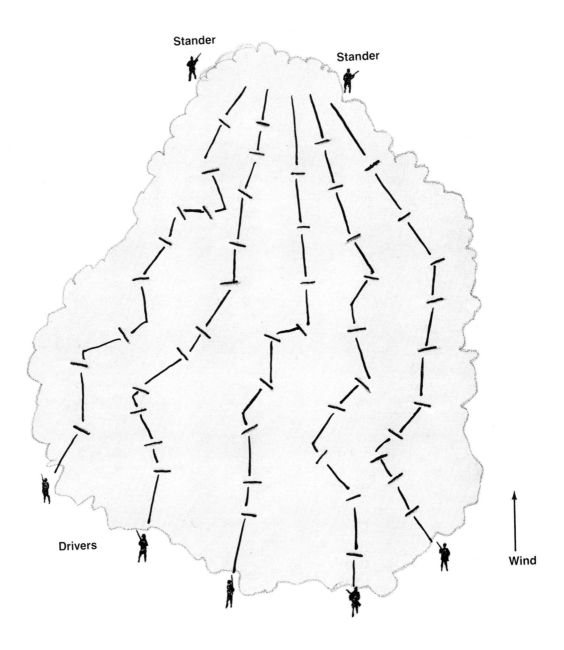

A stillhunt drive is set up like this. Two standers cover the downwind (narrow) end, and all other hunters begin stillhunting and driving from the upwind end. Each driver zigs and zags, and checks all available cover in stops and starts. This drive is best suited to larger areas which are impossible to drive with one or two men.

there simply are too many holes for a buck to slip through. The secret to this hunting method is to position as many people as possible on the upwind side of the cover and one or two standers on the downwind side.

The standers move into position early, and then wait for something to come their way. In reality, drivers more often score on bucks than do the standers and the reason is simple once we analyze our strategy.

We position our drivers in a semi-circle at the top (upwind) end of the cover to be driven, and then each driver slowly stillhunts downwind. Each takes a few steps, stops and looks in all directions before moving again.

It's impossible to move too slowly in a stillhunt drive; it may require two or three hours to cover one-third to one-half a mile of prime whitetail habitat. Each hunter investigates each draw, ravine or gully in his area. The trick is to poke along while investigating blowdowns and other cover. Move slowly, try to anticipate where a deer may be bedded down and attempt to position yourself in a place from which you can shoot an escaping buck.

Whitetail bucks often will hear a stillhunter approaching, and only when that hunter gets close will the deer get up and begin moving. There's a possibility that once a buck starts moving it will blunder into another driver as he stillhunts nearby.

Even if shots are fired the stillhunt drivers should continue in the downwind direction in hopes of pushing out deer to the standers. Keep moving, keep looking and perhaps someone will get a shot.

The reason for lengthy pauses is to give a moving deer a chance to cross in front of another driver. One whiff of scent from that hunter may spook the buck in front of another sportsman who may get a decent shot.

Stillhunt drives produce on occasion, and at other times fail to deliver even one buck sighting. But, if all drives were destined for success then we'd have far fewer whitetails than currently inhabit the North American continent.

CHAPTER 8

Guns and Loads for Deer

A whitetail deer isn't a terribly big animal. The average whitetail weighs somewhere between 100 and 150 pounds, and a critter this size doesn't require a lot of killing. Sure, an outsized whitetail with an obvious thyroid problem may tip the scales at 200 pounds, and on occasion a monster buck may hit the 300-pound mark, but the chances of a hunter encountering such heavyweights are indeed rare.

Most deer hunters gun in areas where whitetails are of average size and choose their firearms accordingly. A Winchester .458 Magnum for whitetail deer is extreme overkill in my estimation, and a .22 Long Rifle veers off in the other direction as a whitetail deer cartridge. You don't need an elephant gun to drill holes through deerskin, and you shouldn't suffer brutal recoil. Big rifles just aren't needed.

My argument for the proper firearm and cartridge in this book is to use that which will competently place the bullet in the proper place, at the proper time, while doing enough damage to the nervous system and vital organs to kill the deer quickly.

The lowly .22 rifle has probably popped more whitetails in rural areas than any other, but this gun is not legal in any state or province I know. It is most often used by poachers who steal our game by spotlighting and shooting the animals at night. So, right off, we eliminate the .22 and relegate it to the rabbit and squirrel woods where it belongs.

At the other end of the scale are those folks with an Elmer Keith syndrome. I met Elmer many years ago and marveled at his big-bore philosophy. Mind you, I didn't agree with him and his "wham, bam, slap 'em down" theory, but I did respect his opinions and his rights to use whatever cannon or miniature howitzer that was in vogue at the time.

I've seen a few lads toting smokepoles in the whitetail woods that would have made a Kodiak bear hightail it into the nearest Devil's club thicket. On the other hand, I've seen hunters use a bullet too small or of the wrong configuration for deer, and one is as bad as the other in my mind.

Ask 100 authors of deer-hunting books the burning question, "What cartridge, firearm, bullet weight and bullet configuration is best for whitetail deer?" and you'll probably receive 100 different answers. Simply stated: There is no best all-round cartridge or firearm for whitetail deer for all occasions. What works in one area, and under one specific set of circumstances, may not work in another location.

Look at it this way. Let's say you hunt whitetail deer in the Montana mountains, and you need a flat-shooting rifle capable of hitting a whitetail buck across a mountain valley. You're not going to hunt with iron sights and a 30/30 carbine shooting a bullet with the trajectory of a last-second basketball shot from midcourt. You'll be toting a rifle—probably a bolt action—that whips out a bullet at 2,750 to 3,000 or more feet per second. You'll probably opt for a .264 Magnum, .270, 7mm Magnum or 30-06 and a light bullet.

But, for sake of ending the eternal firearm argument where losers often wind up with a bloody nose, let's say you are hunting a cedar swamp in the Midwest or deep South. Who needs a flat-shooter? Not you or me. We want a midrange thumper which will shoot out to 50 yards.

Anyone who hunts where the shooting distance is measured by yards rather than as far as you can see will want something that hits on target, has the necessary knockdown power and is easy to carry. Those of us who hunt such areas care little about being burdened down with a 10-pound-plus scoped rifle that can shoot eyes out of squirrels at 300 yards. We want a lightweight, easy-to-carry rifle that will come to the shoulder fast, is easily sighted on the target and which, when the trigger is pulled, will dump a whitetail buck. We care little for fancy engraving, and gold triggers or inlays mean nothing. These guns will get battered and beat up, and will look like we've used them to drive fence posts by the end of a season. We want reliable firearms which do the job for which they were intended, and that is to shoot whitetails at reasonably close ranges.

Conversely, a firearm shooting a bullet with a curving trajectory is of little use in the prairie or mountain states. Hunters who gun whitetail bucks in the open spaces want, and need, something which will pop a buck at long ranges. They want scoped rifles instead of iron sights, and they want a flat-shooter that will shoot—and knock down—a buck at eye-straining distances.

So, this chapter is not meant to promote differences of opinion or to toss a white-gloved challenge in the face of opponents. It is meant to stress the obvious; use a firearm that will do the job for which it was intended, at the range for which it was intended, in the most expedient manner possible.

It means to choose the firearm that's right for you, and correct for the country and terrain being hunted. Nothing more, nothing less.

I'm a firm believer in the proper gun and load for the area. I often carry four or five

A flat-shooting rifle like this Smith & Wesson Model 1500 is good for hunting fringeland deer.

A midrange thumper like Herb Boldt's .35 Remington is suitable where shots average about 50 yards. He uses a scope on his rifle to spot holes in the brush through which he'll shoot.

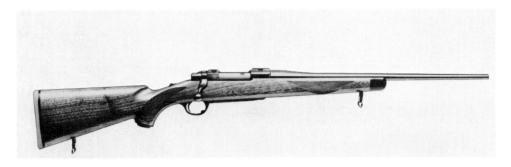

A lightweight rifle which comes to the shoulder fast, like this 6-pound 30/30 Ruger bolt action, is a gun to use in tight spots or heavy cover.

Claude Pollington uses a flat-shooting, scoped .270 bolt-action rifle when hunting the open places.

firearms on a hunting trip. My arsenal, if you will, consists of a Model 70 .270 Winchester, a Model 70 (pre-1964) Winchester .264 Magnum, a Remington 870 in 3-inch magnum 12 gauge with an 18-inch barrel or 28-inch modified barrel (or a Smith & Wesson Model 3000 Police Shotgun in 12 gauge), a Ruger .44 Magnum carbine and a Smith & Wesson Model 469 9mm semiautomatic loaded with hardball rounds. On occasion I'll carry a Winchester Model 94 30-30 carbine, and it has smacked down several whitetail bucks for me during hunts in brushy country.

Which of these guns do I use most of the time? The answer is easy—none of them. Oh, I hunt whitetail deer nearly every day of the Michigan season, and in several other states and provinces as well, but this is my standard arsenal. I pick and choose firearms according to the terrain I'm hunting at the time. No one firearm does yeoman service for me; instead, I may carry two, three or four different firearms at different times each day as circumstances and terrain dictate. No one firearm can do everything you demand of it; some may pass muster on most occasions, and others will fill the bill only under specific circumstances. The choice is yours.

Go with whatever is right for the terrain being hunted, and choose a reliable firearm. But, whatever you do, choose a gun that will shoot where you want and be extremely familiar with it before you enter the deer woods.

I firmly believe that the pill you push out the barrel of a deer rifle must be up to the job. It must enter the vital area of a whitetail, expand rapidly and produce tremendous shocking power while doing considerable damage to internal organs. Properly placed, the correct bullet will do the job.

A full-jacketed bullet has little place in the deer woods unless the hunter is skilled enough to take brain or spine shots. Body shots with full-jacketed bullets often result in wounded deer getting away.

I see many hunters using Silvertip bullets on whitetails. These bullets were designed for thick-skinned animals and dangerous critters such as big bears. Granted, Silvertips in one cartridge or another have dropped many bucks down through the years, but, in my opinion, they are an inferior choice.

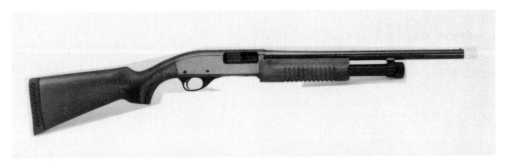

A Smith & Wesson Model 3000 Police Shotgun is effective for driving thick cover or when on stand where shots are close.

Round-nose bullets have had many admirers over the years due to their supposed "brush-busting" abilities. Those in favor of heavy, round-nose slugs claim they will bust through brush and retain their direction.

Nonsense.

Any bullet, regardless of configuration or design, on encountering a twig, sapling or low-growing brushy cover will ricochet away from the target. If the bullet hits the sapling dead-center, it generally disintegrates.

What bullet styles do I like? I use nothing but hollow points or pointed soft points for whitetail deer.

I'm a firm believer in the 240-grain hollow point in my Ruger .44 Mag, and I stuff my .264 Mangle'um full of 100-grain hollow points for those mid- or long-range shots. My .270 shucks out 100-grain hollow points, and all have anchored deer with one shot. If I'm going to shoot a whitetail buck, which I do each year, I don't like to chase 'em to hell and gone over ridges and through swamp because of poor bullet performance on thin-skinned animals. I want, and expect, instant results when I squeeze the trigger.

The above loads perform well for me wherever I hunt. They open up immediately upon penetrating the hide of a buck, and they do their job inside the animal instead of expending their energy and mushrooming qualities after having passed through the deer.

Mind you, I've nothing against reloading. I've reloaded for years, and find great pleasure in doing so but I use factory loads when hunting. I like to reload, and down through the years have used Nosler, Speer, Norma, Sierra and other bullets, but when the chips are down and I want venison in my freezer I use factory loads.

I'm only human, and as such can make a mistake when reloading. I'd hate to miss the buck of a lifetime due to my error. Therefore, when I go hunting I stuff Federal, Remington or Winchester hulls in my rifle.

There are any number of excellent deer rifles and cartridges on today's market. They are, however, only good when the hunter knows how to shoot and is capable of putting the bullet where it counts.

This means familiarity with the rifle, and it means sighting it in properly. One common problem among many deer hunters is they seldom touch their rifle until the day before the season opens, and then they will twist off two or three rounds and call it good enough.

Well, damn it, it's not good enough. A whitetail deer is an amazing animal, and as such should be afforded better treatment than to be gutshot by some dude who cranked off three rounds at a pine stump and managed to hit it once. The proper deer rifle should be able to hit dead on at the ranges you expect to be shooting, and the hunter should be capable of placing a bullet where he wants—every time.

Years ago I worked in a sporting goods store. My job, for the six weeks preceding Michigan's deer season, was to sight in a variety of rifles for customers. Many would buy a scope for their centerfire banger, bring it to me and ask for it to be sighted in.

I did the job because it was my job, but I cautioned each hunter to shoot the rifle himself. I would offer to work with them, and chanted how they probably would look through the scope differently than I would and this could cause their shot to go high, low or off to one side and result in a miss, or worse, a wounding shot.

I didn't get through to one man in a hundred. Most were too lazy to do it themselves, and then would gripe to me after the season when they missed a buck. All I guaranteed was their rifle would be sighted in, but it would be sighted in according to how I held the rifle and looked through the glass. I'd guarantee the rifle to be on (for me), and to hit on the paper and nothing else. That was good enough for most of them.

Down through the years I developed a method which would accurately sight in most rifles with nine shots ... maximum. I heartily advise any hunter to sight in his own rifle, and to use this system. Learn your firearm, and know what it will do. Some rifles shoot high or low, or off to one side or the other, after one or two shots and this is something each hunter should know ... before hunting season starts.

Here's how I sighted in up to 200 rifles each fall. It worked then, and it will work now for you.

Sight in a Rifle with Nine Shots

You say you missed a standing shot at ol' Mossy Horns last year? And at 25 yards, no less.

If this happened to you, and you wish to correct the problem before the next hunting season, don't despair. With just 30 minutes of your time, and nine cartridges for your rifle, we'll do something about it right now. You'll have to do the sighting in yourself, but it will be good practice.

Simply remember that no two people hold and shoot a rifle the same way, and no two people look through a scope in the same manner. Head positions on the gunstock vary from one hunter to another, and the only way in which a gun can be accurately sighted in is if you shoot it yourself. Dodge the issue, and get someone else to sight in the rifle, and you're missing the boat and probably will miss the deer.

Most hunters use a scope on their deer rifle, and this technique is designed for just those people. This procedure is not meant to be used with iron sights.

Many sportsmen feel all scoped rifles will hit a target at 100 yards. It's true if the rifle is properly sighted in and untrue if the rifle is not. I've seen rifles with which I couldn't hit the inside of a barn I was standing in without proper sighting-in techniques. Nothing, and I mean nothing, is more disconcerting with a new (or old) rifle than to pop off a string of shots at 100 yards, walk down to the target and find that not a single bullet cut the paper.

I've learned the best way to sight in a rifle is to begin at a 25-yard range. Don shooting earmuffs, get a firm rest at the shooting bench, place a soft sandbag under the fore-end of the rifle and aim directly at the bull's-eye.

The next step is important. Take a deep breath, let it all the way out and squeeze the trigger. Don't jerk it, and do your best not to flinch. Fire three shots at a very slow pace to allow the barrel to cool between shots. Warm barrels can cause bullets to wander, and most shots at whitetails will be from a cold barrel.

Once you've fired three shots walk to the target and circle the bullet holes with a black felt-tip pen. Use a ruler, and measure from the center of your group to the center of the bullseye. This is the distance you must adjust the scope's elevation and windage dials.

If you've carefully taken aim, and slowly squeezed off each of three shots with ample time between each to cool the barrel, all shots should be within 1 or 2 inches at the 25-yard range.

Make the necessary adjustments, up or down, left or right, and consult the directions issued with the scope. Most scopes adjust at a quarter, half or minute-of-angle (one inch at 100 yards) per click, but many scope manufacturers use a different scale. Compute your changes to correspond to a 100-yard range, and erect the target at that distance.

Let's pretend our rifle gave a sample grouping at 25 yards by being 3 inches low and 2 inches to the right. At 25 yards we'll have to multiply by four to get the proper sighting at 100 yards in order to make the correct adjustments.

If your scope has ¼ minute-of-angle clicks you'll have to move the elevation dial 12 clicks up (four times 3 inches) and to the left 8 clicks (four times 2 inches). This should bring the point of impact very close to the bull's-eye at 100 yards with a good rest.

Now take another firm rest and fire three evenly spaced shots at the bull's-eye at 100 yards with a lengthy pause between shots to allow for barrel cooling. Take the pen and ruler, and walk to the target and measure from the center of the grouping to the bull's-eye. All three shots should again be in a circle of two or three inches or less.

It's time to make final adjustments for elevation and windage. If your scope is calibrated to ¼-inch clicks, four clicks will move the point of impact one inch at 100 yards. If calibrated in ½-inch clicks two clicks will move it one inch at 100 yards.

Don't guess at the clicks, but count each one as you turn the dial. A dime or screwdriver will work, and many dials have knurled wheels which can be turned with fingertip pressure. Make these final adjustments with care, and don't hurry the process.

Fire three more careful shots from the shooting bench. If you've done everything that needs to be done you should be right on the money.

Because the line of sight through a scope is somewhat higher than the bore, this causes the bullet to cross the line of sight twice from muzzle to target. A rifle sighted in at 100 yards to hit at point of aim will also be at point of aim at about 25 yards.

Many hunters, and rightly so, will sight in scoped rifles to hit 3 inches high at 100 yards. A flat-shooting rifle sighted in three inches high at 100 yards will hit at point of aim at 25 yards and again somewhere between 200 and 250 yards. It will be shooting about an inch high at 50 yards, three inches high at 100 yards, one and one-half inches high at 175 yards and dead on at 200–250 yards.

Some hunters, if they know a shot will be taken inside of 60 yards, will sight their scoped rifle in to hit dead-on at that range. Any deer which appears between muzzle length and 60 yards can be hit by holding the scope's reticule directly on the target.

This method of sighting in a scoped rifle is easy. There is nothing mysterious about sighting in a rifle, and the job is best done by the person who will be shooting it. Become familiar with the rifle, and practice shooting it several times before deer season.

Thirty minutes or less of your time spent sighting in your favorite rifle can spell the difference between eating venison steaks this fall and grilled hamburgers. How well you shoot, and whether you score, will depend on how well the rifle is sighted in and how much you practice with it at various distances before deer season opens.

Guns and Loads

It's often been said that any caliber rifle bullet will kill a whitetail deer, and exponents of that theory will get little argument from me. But, just because a given caliber and bullet will dump a nice buck for one person doesn't mean it is capable of standing up to continued use from the majority of the hunting fraternity.

The following, from smallest caliber to largest, are my recommendations for whitetail deer.

Cartridge	Bullet Weight	Bullet Type	Muzzle Velocity
270 Winchester	130 grains	BTSP	3110
7mm Remington Magnum	125 grains	PPSP	3310
7mm Remington Magnum	150 grains	PPSP	3110
7mm Remington Magnum	175 grains	PPSP	2860
30–30 Winchester	125 grains	HP	2570
30–30 Winchester	150 grains	OPE	2390
30–30 Winchester	170 grains	HPCL	2200
300 Savage	150 grains	PPSP	2630
308 Winchester	110 grains	PSP	3180
308 Winchester	125 grains	PSP	3050
308 Winchester	150 grains	PPSP	2820
30–06 Springfield	110 grains	PSP	3380
30–06 Springfield	125 grains	PSP	3140
30–06 Springfield	150 grains	PPSP	2920
300 Winchester Magnum	150 grains	PPSP	3290
303 British	180 grains	PPSP	2460
35 Remington	150 grains	PSPCL	2300
44–40 Winchester	200 grains	SP	1190
44 Winchester Magnum	240 grains	SP, SJHP	1760

Cartridge	Bullet Weight	Bullet Type	Muzzle Velocity
44 Winchester Magnum	240 grains	HSP	1760
444 Marlin	240 grains	SP	2350
222 Remington Magnum	55 grains	PSP	3240
222 Remington Magnum	55 grains	HPPL	3240
223 Remington	55 grains	PSP	3240
22–250 Remington	55 grains	PSP	3730
243 Winchester	85 grains	BTHP	3320
243 Winchester	100 grains	SP	2960
6mm Remington	80 grains	PSP	3470
6mm Remington	100 grains	PPSP	3130
25–06 Remington	87 grains	HPPL	3440
25–06 Remington	117 grains	SP	3060
6.5mm Remington Mag.	120 grains	PSPCL	3210
264 Winchester Magnum	100 grains	PSP	3320
264 Winchester Magnum	140 grains	PPSP	3030
270 Winchester	100 grains	PSP	3480
270 Winchester	130 grains	PPSP	3110

Abbreviations for the various bullet types listed above include: HP—Hollow Point; SP—Soft Point, PEP—Pointed Expanding Point; JHP—Jacketed Hollow Point; PP—Power Point; SJHP—Semi-Jacketed Hollow Point; BTHP—Boat Tail Hollow Point; HPPL—Hollow Point Power-Lokt; PPSP—Power Point Soft Point; OPE—Opening Point Expanding; HPCL—Hollow Point Core Lokt and PSPCL—Pointed Soft Point Core Lokt.

Note that hundreds of different bullets in various calibers and configurations are available from manufacturers of reloading supplies. All offer fine bullets in weights unavailable from arms manufacturers.

Handgun Loads for Deer

A handgun for whitetail deer represents a big challenge for some folks. The handgun (preferably scoped) needed to down a buck at ranges from 40 to 100 yards is indeed a handful. Such guns beller and bark, but in the hands of an expert they offer deadly accuracy, sufficient knockdown power and reasonably mild recoil if MagnaPorted.

Granted, a whitetail handgun isn't for everyone. Outfit one with a scope and the rig takes on enough weight as to be uncomfortable to carry in one hand. Larry Kelly of MagnaPort Arms in Mt. Clemens, Michigan, is an advocate of handguns for deer. He often uses a sling attached to the butt and barrel of his handgun, and with one of several hand-held cannons of various calibers has managed to drop elephants, lions, other assorted and sundry African beasties and more than a few deer in his native Michigan.

"Laws vary from state to state, but U.S. residents may not take handguns into Canada for any purpose," states Kelly. "I do not recommend using a .25, .32, or .38 Special handgun for deer hunting. Even the .357 Magnum is marginal in my opinion.

"A handgun can be extremely accurate, but the use of one for hunting deer means constant practice. A hunter should be able to consistently place six shots in a pie plate at ranges from 25 to 100 yards, and if he can't . . . well, he should either practice more or consider using a centerfire rifle."

Kelly believes that the sportsman must determine the exact distance at which he can accurately shoot, and then practice at that range. He believes a scoped pistol or revolver will increase any handgunner's ability to place an accurate shot on a whitetail buck, and a rest to steady the aim is a good hedge against misses.

"My choice for a hunting handgun is a .41 or .44 Magnum, and the latter is my favorite," Kelly says. "I recomend a full metal-jacketed bullet in either caliber, but a jacketed soft-point bullet will work. Don't scrimp on barrel length; a 5-inch or longer barrel is preferred, and I attach a sling for easy carrying."

Kelly's firm specializes in MagnaPorting pistol, revolver and rifle barrels to cut down on muzzle jump and to enable hunters to get on target faster if a second shot is needed. This process reduces recoil by about 30 percent, eliminates most of the muzzle jump "and it enables hunters to recover that much faster."

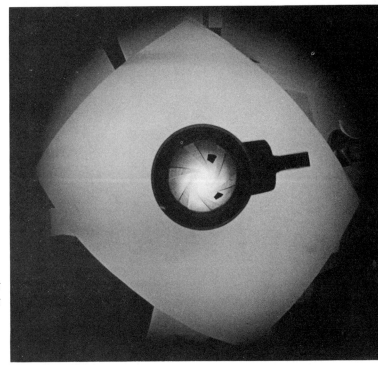

MagnaPorting, as shown here, reduces muzzle jump and recoil in handguns, rifles and shotguns.

Larry Kelly, owner of MagnaPort, downed this nice buck with a MagnaPorted and scoped Thompson/Center Contender in .44 Magnum caliber.

Kelly deer hunts from a blind or on stand, and tries to position himself so if a buck crosses his field of fire he will have a broadside shot at the animal. He feels hunters should aim for the center of mass (the vital heart-lung area), and avoid neck shots except at close range. He feels neck shots increase the chance of a handgunner wounding and eventually losing the deer.

Single-shot pistol, single or double-action wheelgun (revolver) or semiautomatic—the choice is up to the hunter. I dumped a small buck last year with a Smith & Wesson

Model 469 in 9mm loaded with hardball ammo, but most serious aficionados lean toward larger handguns. The single-shot Thompson/Center Contender is a solid choice among many, and heavy revolvers like Colt, Smith & Wesson and Ruger offer a wide choice of single- or double-action revolvers in various barrel lengths. Few serious handgunners use semiautomatics unless they are in law enforcement and wish to hunt with their traditional sidearm.

A handgun hunter should be able to place six shots into a pie plate at ranges from 25 to 100 yards. Ted Nugent can.

MagnaPorting heavy handguns like Ted Nugent's .44 Magnum helps tame the piece somewhat, and enables you to get on target faster for a second shot if needed.

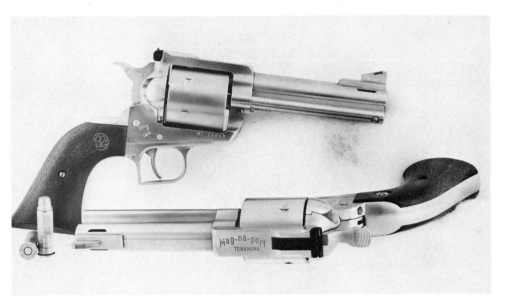

Heavy magnum handguns like these MagnaPort Tomahawks in .44 Magnum caliber are needed for whitetail deer hunting.

The following cartridges and bullet styles will work for handgun deer hunters:

HANDGUN LOADS

Cartridge	Bullet Weight	Bullet Type	Muzzle Velocity
256 Winchester Mag.	60 grains	HP	2350
357 Magnum	150 grains	FMJ	1600
357 Magnum	158 grains	JHP	1450
9mm Luger	125 grains	MC	1120
243 Winchester	85 grains	BTHP	Approx. 3320
243 Winchester	100 grains	PPSP	Approx. 2960
270 Winchester	100 grains	PSP	Approx. 3480
30–30 Winchester	125 grains	HP	Approx. 2570
30–30 Winchester	150 grains	OPE	Approx. 2390
41 Remington Magnum	210 grains	Lead	1050
41 Remington Magnum	210 grains	SP	1500
44 Remington Magnum	180 grains	JHP	1610
44 Remington Magnum	200 grains	JHP	1650
44 Remington Magnum	240 grains	JSP	1625
44 Remington Magnum	240 grains	SJHP	1180
45 Winchester Magnum	230 grains	FMC	1400

Abbreviations: FMC—Full Metal Case; SJHP—Semi Jacketed Hollow Point; JSP—Jacketed Soft Point; SP—Soft Point; OPE—Open Point Expanding; HP—Hollow Point; JHP—Jacketed Hollow Point; BTHP—Boat Tail Hollow Point; MC—Metal Case; PPSP—Power Point Soft Point.

Note that handgunners have other specialized "wildcat" cartridges available which offer good possibilities. Also note that the muzzle velocities listed above as "approximate" will be considerably less when fired from a shorter-barreled handgun. The muzzle velocities for the so-called rifle cartridges were fired from rifles with a 20- or 24-inch barrel rather than the 5- to 10-inch barrels found on most hunting handguns.

Shotguns and Loads

The ever-present shotgun makes a fine sporting arm for deer hunters, and in many portions of the country (particularly in the heavily populated eastern and midwestern states) a shotgun is the only legal firearm during deer season. Some states allow the use of buckshot, and others do not, but wherever they're legal, buckshot and slugs offer sportsmen a fine alternative to a deer rifle.

Single-shots, double barrels, over-unders, pumps and automatics—all are adequate for deer hunting. The same shotgun used to chase ruffed grouse or bunnies, geese or woodcock, ducks or pheasants will serve admirably in the deer woods. However, with the advent of slugs-only seasons in many states certain firearms manufacturers such as Mossberg, Remington, Smith & Wesson and Winchester have begun manufacturing shotguns designed specifically to shoot rifled slugs. These slug barrels are generally 18 to 20 inches long and have iron sights. A scope can be mounted atop the receiver. (A 4X scope increases the shotgun's effectiveness.) Iron-sighted slug barrels are consistently accurate out to 50 or 60 yards, and a scoped shotgun in the hands of a practiced shot can deliver kills out to 80 yards.

Winchester-Western, Remington-Peters and Federal manufacture rifled slugs, as does Brenneke, a German firm. Slugs are available for shotguns from 10 gauge down to the lowly .410. The .410 is not recommended for whitetails, although a precise shot in a vital area will drop a deer. Most slug guns used for deer fall in the 12- and 20-gauge class; a few hunters use 10-gauge, 16-gauge and .410 slugs.

I've known a few brave souls who have tried to reload shotgun shells with buckshot or slugs. I prefer store-boughts and consider reloads hazardous: when it gets down to the nitty-gritty you want to know your shell will deliver.

I wish I had a dollar for every argument I've heard about which is best for whitetails: single-ought (0), double-ought (00) or triple-ought (000) buckshot for 12-gauge shotguns. There are those who will disagree with Ma Richey's little boy Dave, but I don't use any of the big buckshot loads.

If I'm going to use a cornshucker for deer, and anticipate close (within 30 yards) shots, I'll stuff it full of 3-inch magnum 12-gauge shells loaded with No. 4 buckshot.

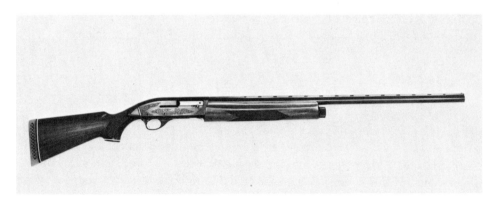

A Smith & Wesson Model 1000 3-inch 12-gauge shotgun is good for deer.

Jack Teegarden carries a 12-gauge double with No. 4 buckshot.

Each of the 41 buck in that round are about the size of a .22 caliber bullet, and they seem to hold together at 30 yards in a tighter pattern, regardless of choke, than 0 or 00 buckshot. The knockdown force of this load at close range is unbelievable. It's deadly on fringeland whitetails.

Of course, in other shotgun gauges, No. 4 buckshot is not available. I wouldn't suggest using this load past 40 yards, and only then in a 3-inch magnum. The 2¾-inch magnum pushes out only 27 pellets, and although it offers a wider spreading pattern than 0, 00 or 000 buckshot, the others may have the edge in the smaller magnum shell.

My advice to shotgun users is to use the maximum number of buckshot pellets in a load commercially available from manufacturers. Do not attempt to handload buckshot or rifled slugs, and whenever possible stick with the heavy magnum load.

BUCKSHOT

Gauge	Length Shell	Powder Dram Equiv.	Shot Size, No.
10	3½	Super Mag.	4 Buck – 54
12	3 Mag.	4½	00 Buck – 15
12	3 Mag.	4½	4 Buck – 41
12	2¾ Mag.	4	1 Buck – 20
12	2¾ Mag.	4	00 Buck – 12
12	2¾	Max.	00 Buck – 9
12	2¾	3¾	0 Buck – 12
12	2¾	Max.	1 Buck – 16
12	2¾	Max.	4 Buck – 27
12	2¾ Mag.	—	000 Buck – 8
12	3 Mag.	—	000 Buck – 10
16	2¾	3	1 Buck – 12
20	2¾	Max.	3 Buck – 20

SLUGS

Gauge	Length Shell	Powder Dram Equiv.	Shot Size, No.
10	3½	Mag.	1¾ oz.
12	2¾	Max.	1¼ oz.
12	2¾	Max.	1 oz.
16	2¾	Max.	⅘ oz.
20	2¾	Max.	⅝ oz.
20	2¾	Max.	¾ oz.
410	2½	Max.	⅕ oz.

Note that the lowly .410 is not offered in buckshot loads, and I can think of no reasonable excuse for using a slug from this tiny shotgun for deer.

You'll note that with the exception of my personal guns, I have not mentioned specific brand names of different rifles and shotguns. That's because I don't think it's necessary. What I say about brand X may not induce you to purchase that model, and this is as it should be.

Chances are that if you are reading this book you already own a rifle or shotgun, perhaps both and possibly one or more of each, and any gun I'd tout would be considered a slap in the face if you happen to favor a different model. Besides, it's not so much which rifle or shotgun you favor that is important; it's what load you use, and where you shoot a deer that counts.

CHAPTER 9

Bowhunting
Fringeland Deer

I've killed whitetail bucks with bow-and-arrow, muzzleloading rifle and shotgun, centerfire rifles, 12-gauge shotguns and handguns. Each animal taken has provided me with good sport and a wholesome day in the deer woods, but the bucks which stay with me and stoke a fire in my memory bank were those taken with a bow.

Robert Traver, the widely acclaimed trout-fishing writer and personal friend, once said, "Trout fishing with a fly is the most fun you can have with your clothes on." He may have a point, but it's my contention that bowhunting for whitetails falls in the same category.

Bowhunting is fun. And it offers a distinct challenge. The bowhunter must be able to approach a high-strung quarry and get within striking distance without being detected; and he must become proficient enough with bow and arrow to consistently hit his target.

Taking a buck with bow isn't easy. If you think a fringeland whitetail buck is spastic, around the bend with nervous energy and always ready to flee because of its inborn tensions, then consider the bowhunter's plight as he tries for a shot. I have shot a great number of whitetails around the North American continent, and I've yet to shed the heart-pounding thrill of seeing a nice buck at spitting distances. So far I've not been able to tame the wildly beating heart, the shortness of breath and the adrenalin rush that sweeps over me when I know a bow shot is imminent. It's just not the same with a rifle or shotgun.

I'm convinced that bowhunters are better hunters simply because of the limited range of their chosen weapon. It takes nerves of steel to sit out the gaze of a buck who knows something is out of place, and it takes internal reserves to resist the temptation to loft an arrow at a nice buck at 40 yards when with patience a 20-yard shot is possible.

The bowhunter often must sit motionless, operate around errant breezes which may carry his scent to deer, allow numerous does and fawns (and, yes, perhaps even smaller bucks) to pass before coming to full draw on a nice buck.

Bowhunting whitetail deer has increased in the past ten years, and bowhunter numbers will probably double in the years to come. The advent of the compound bow, and now the programmed or cam compound, has been the major factor in weaning hunters from their rifles and shotguns.

It takes nerves of steel to hold off shooting with a bow until a buck is within range. A treestand helped this hunter get above the animal.

A bowhunter must resist taking long shots, and instead wait for the deer to get close. This snow-camo-clad bowhunter (left and opposite) uses a compound bow. Note glove on left hand, and finger tabs on the right.

Which Bow for You?

The job of selecting a bow boils down to spending your money and taking your chances. It helps to take advice from other hunters, and there are a few rules to follow which can make bow selection easier.

Many first-time bow buyers walk into the local sporting goods store or archery shop, and examine the gleaming products as if they were judging a hunting rifle. They "ooh" and "ah" over the finish, the marvelous grain of the wood, seldom realizing the wood will be covered with stick-on camo tape, spray painted with camo paint or enclosed in a camo bow sock to hide the shiny finish.

Hunting bows fall into three basic categories—recurves, straight or compound bows.

Most hunting bows sold today are compounds. They have pulleys and eccentric wheels which offer a certain degree of let-off (lack of poundage being held) when pulled to full draw. Few recurves or straight bows are sold for hunting purposes.

Let-off generally is either 30 or 50 percent, depending on the bow model, and this means a reduction in effort needed to hold the bowstring (and arrow) at full draw. A 60-pound-pull compound, with a 30 percent let-off, will feature a reduction of approximately 18 pounds or a bowhunter hold of only 42 pounds once the bow is fully drawn.

A 50-percent let-off, with a 60-pound bow, will mean the bowhunter is holding back only 30 pounds at full draw. Obviously, for guys like me who have repeatedly failed the Charles Atlas and Vic Tanny courses, a 50-percent let-off allows us to use a slightly

heavier draw-weight than we would with a recurve bow. Those of you who are amply endowed with bulging biceps will be able to handle a 30-percent let-off compound bow.

Determine what comes with the bow. Does it have a Burger Button or just a little Mickey Mouse arrow rest with a knob that serves as a Burger Button? Is the bow handle wood or magnesium? If it's the latter plan on hunting only during warm weather because a metal handle will freeze your fingers during cold-weather hunts. What kind of arrow rest does your new-found love possess? Cheap, relatively expensive or expensive? Arrow rests are personal, too, and a good one is best.

The bow for an avid bowhunter is a functional thing. It's comparable to a car used to carry fishermen along two-tracks to a secluded beaverpond for brook trout. The bow is to be used, and not hung on a rack to admire.

What you see is what you get. All the glitter, fancy words on advertisements or cheap doodads will not help you shoot a buck with a bow. Select a good bow—one you can shoot—and you'll score on a whitetail providing you are as good a woodsman and hunter as you are a bowshot. Choose a fancy bow, and neglect your hunting skills and you'll be an also-ran in the deer woods.

One final tip about bows: The best bow made in the free world won't kill a whitetail deer unless you know how to hunt. Too many sportsmen practice constantly on paper targets until they can stack arrows, but still they fail to shoot deer. Given my druthers I'd rather hunt with a guy who practices just enough to know where his arrow is going rather than one who can hit the bull's-eye every time but doesn't have a clue where to shoot a deer.

Arrows

Arguing arrows and arrow length or fletchings versus plastic vanes is like heatedly discussing politics or religion. There are no winners—only losers. When I want to know about these things, I consult a chart published by Easton Aluminum. If I know my draw length and the pound-pull of my bow, I can make a wise arrow selection.

Arrow shafts are available in aluminum, fiberglass, graphite and wood. Wooden arrows are almost a thing of the past, but I've used them for years with my compound bow.

"Hell fire, man, don't you know that wood arrows shot from a compound can do bad things to you?" someone will ask. Sure, I've heard horror stories of wood arrows breaking on release and inserting themselves into the bow hand or wrist but it's never happened to me. A properly seasoned, straight and finely tuned wood shaft is just as safe when shot from a compound bow as from a recurve. The only problem is many bowhunters don't know it.

This is not meant to be an advertisement for wood arrows because in reality I shoot aluminum 95 percent of the time from my compound bow. Just realize that with caution, wood arrows will work just as well from a compound as from a recurve. Pundits may call me down on this, but I believe wood arrows strike the target with more force than aluminum arrows. Note the term "arrow" refers to shafts with feather fletching or plastic vanes installed, while "shafts" refer to the aluminum arrow tubing minus feathers or fletching.

Arguments flare back and forth like an out-of-control brush fire about the advantages of using a lighter arrow for slightly more speed versus a heavier arrow for better penetration. The Easton Aluminum Arrow Chart, available at any archery shop, explains it quite well; at each draw length and actual bow weight are a choice of one, two, three or four different arrow sizes. Consult the chart, and ask your dealer's advice, to determine which arrow weight will be best for you.

For instance: I shoot a 29-inch arrow from a bow set at 58 pounds. A quick glance at the chart indicates I should choose an aluminum arrow designated 2213 (473 grains), 2117 (535 grains) or 2018 (542 grains). If my shooting style and preference leaned toward a lighter, slightly faster arrow I'd opt for the 2213. However, if I wanted an arrow with slightly more weight (which I do) to deliver a bit better penetration I'd choose the 2018 (which is what I shoot).

I've seen countless bowhunters purchase the most expensive bow available, spend hard-earned bucks on sights and rests, and slather money hither and yon on other bowhunting accessories. Then they make a major mistake by skimping on arrow quality.

Fishermen have long known that fishing line is the main connection between rod and angler and the fish, and they know to skimp on cheap line is an unwise investment. Two many bowhunters fail to heed this lesson and spend ten bucks on El Cheapo arrows, then wonder why they miss a standing shot at a big buck.

My advice is to purchase the best arrow possible. Arrows run, depending on brand name and locale, anywhere from $12 to $35 per dozen. I generally shoot Easton XX75 Camo Shafts. I've also used Easton Gamegetters and Easton's XX75 Gold arrows, but I prefer a camouflaged arrow with a flame orange or pink nock to help me follow the arrow in flight.

Feathers or plastic vanes—that is the question. Feathers are slightly more forgiving of hunter error or a poor release, but they can be a mess when used in rain or snow although I always use feathers. Plastic vanes work well for most hunters, and hold up in bad weather.

Arrows are commonly sold in dozen lots. I buy twelve arrows of the same brand, length and spine weight and a dozen broadheads of the same type. Six of these arrows are used to practice with some various positions and elevations, and six are carried on my bow quiver.

There's a lesson, I feel, in the above paragraph. Note I said a dozen arrows and broadheads evenly divided between target and hunting arrows. Nowhere up above did I mention using target points for practicing; I practice only with my hunting broadheads.

Broadheads

Broadheads and target points often hit at different points of impact even with the same anchor point and release. It makes little difference to my way of thinking whether you hunt from the ground or a treestand; your point of aim will always be about 3 feet off the ground when shooting at a deer.

With this thought in mind I had a trucker bring a big load of sand into my backyard several years ago for use as a backstop. I position my lifesize deer target where I want it, and shoot broadheads into the sand pile. Sure, it dulls the broadhead, but it builds confidence. It helps to know where the broadhead-tipped arrow will hit, and only through practice in this manner can a hunter be assured of accurate shots.

There are any number of broadheads on the market. Many will weigh between 115 grains and 140 grains. A few huge heads like the Zonker, Snuffer and others may weigh up to 200 grains.

For many years I used wood shafts with the extra-wide Zonker broadhead. It cut a swath through an animal, and the blood trail was easy to follow. However, since I shoot only 58 pounds at 29 inches my wood arrows with the heavy broadhead would start tailing off at any distance over 30 yards. I now use the aluminum arrows men-

Roger Kerby shooting at a running-deer target sliding down a wire in front of a pile of sand. He practices daily with broadheads.

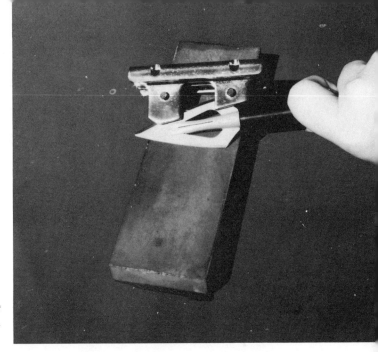

I use an arrow vise and whetstone to put the finishing touches on my Bear broadheads once I work them with a flat file.

tioned earlier, and the time-tested Bear broadhead. These heads are sharper now when they come from the factory than years ago, but I still sharpen them to my liking. A flat file, and five minutes for each broadhead, brings them to razor sharpness.

One important thing to remember: broadheads kill through hemorrhage as they slice through arteries, capillaries and veins. There is little or no shock value to a broadhead hit, and to kill through blood loss the broadhead must be razor sharp. To prevent rust, I coat my sharpened broadheads with 3-in-1 oil, WD 40 or even a very thin layer of Vaseline petroleum jelly.

Many hunters prefer not to sharpen broadheads, and there are any number of companies which produce heads with replaceable blades. A few I'm very familiar with include the Satellite (3- and 4-bladed), Anderson 245 Magnum, Thunderhead, Brute (3- and 4-bladed), Kolpin Modular (3- and 4- and 6-bladed), Wasp (3- and 4-bladed), Rocky Mountain (3- and 4-bladed), Savora and Viper (3- and 4-bladed). If I've missed a few models, it's just because I'm not familiar with all broadhead makes.

Buy a dozen broadheads and arrows, and use six to hunt with and six for practice. Learn how the arrow and broadhead fly at different distances, and practice constantly at varying yardages.

Proper Form

It's one thing to practice with bow and arrow, and still another to do it right. Proper practice means using the proper form, and this will differ slightly from one individual to another. What works for one person may not for the next because of build, facial features, length of arms and many other factors.

George Gardner, an archery tackle representative, has spent hours with me in order to develop good shooting habits. He advises to be consistent, and to choose the same anchor point time and again.

"The most common anchor point for bowhunters," Gardner maintains, "is the corner of the mouth. But, the hunter must hold his bow the same way on each shot and touch the corner of the mouth each time while making the same release time after time. It's not easy."

He suggests grasping the bow like you were reaching out to shake hands. This automatically turns the inside of the elbow to a more vertical position, and this very act will in most cases remove any possibility of an "idiot mark." An idiot mark results from the bow string slapping against the inside of the upper arm, elbow or lower arm. These string slaps are painful, can cause flinching and can be avoided by holding the bow properly or by using an arm guard.

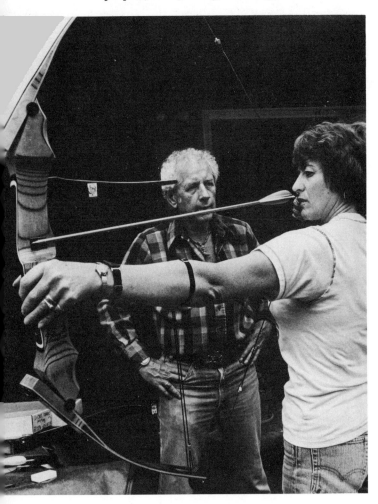

George Gardner (background) observes Kay Richey's shooting form. He specifically checks to see if her anchor point remains the same shot after shot.

"The first step after determining where the nocking point should be (this can be done at any archery shop)," Gardner says, "is to come up with a firm, never-changing anchor point. I advise hunters to lock the web between thumb and forefinger behind the jawbone. Once the fingers draw the arrow back to full draw, and the webbing is locked behind the corner of the jaw you've almost got a rock-solid anchor.

"The next step is to curl the tip of your index finger into the corner of your mouth. This use of thumb and forefinger webbing, corner of jawbone and corner of the mouth gives you a constant anchoring point time after time."

This section on proper form would be inadequate if we didn't discuss the proper stance. The average archer stands to shoot at his target, and this is fine and dandy. The right-handed archer turns his left side slightly toward the target, comes to full draw and firm anchor and lets it rip.

George Gardner checks the nocking point on Kay Richey's bow, and fine-tunes it for her.

Great, as far as it goes. I just question how many bowhunters can stand with feet on the ground and take dog shots at nice bucks. Much of the time when we hunt on the ground we'll be sitting, and if we're in a treestand we may sit or stand. There's too many variables involved for most hunters to always practice shooting the same way.

I mostly sit in treestands. I believe it reduces my silhouette even though I'm hunting from an elevated position. When I hunt on the ground I'm often sitting, and the shots can be awkward at best.

Proper bowhunting form is demonstrated by premier big-buck hunter Paul Mickey. He is shown shooting at targets from an elevated platform in his backyard.

Climbing into a treestand with a bow and broadheads is risky. Jacqui Nathan pulls her bow up after getting into position.

Good form for bowhunters is far different from good form for target archers. If you've done your preseason scouting properly you'll know from which direction a buck should appear, and you'll have your body positioned properly for a shot in that direction.

Learn to position your body properly, and learn to practice shooting at targets from the elevation used while hunting or from ground level in a simulated blind. Nothing is more humbling than to be unable to shoot at a buck because of poor body placement.

And, if you don't believe anything else about bowhunting for fringeland whitetails, believe this: It's one thing to be able to come to full draw with a hunting-weight bow while standing, but it's a different can of worms to do it while bundled up against the cold or while sitting down.

I remember one November when the rut was in full swing. It was cold ... damn cold. My treestand overlooked a trail used by rutting bucks, and I'd seen a nice eight-pointer working the trail daily for a week. He always came just before dark, and seemed to mosey along the trail in an indifferent manner until he came to his scrape line 50 yards away.

I sat and waited, and an hour and then two dragged by. It was fifteen minutes before dark when I saw my buck swagger down the trail. When his head went behind a nearby tree I raised by bow, and started to come to full draw.

The bow string wouldn't budge. I was too cold, and my muscles too cramped to draw the bow. I slowly lowered the bow, flexed my muscles slightly and tried again.

I still couldn't break the 58-pound compound. I couldn't get the string far enough back to take it over the hump, and I had to let the bow down again. By this time the buck knew something was amiss, and was staring intently at my treestand.

I didn't move, and minutes later he started past my stand. I allowed him to pass and tried to come to full draw again. I struggled, gritted my teeth, the arrow fell off the rest and onto my finger and made a slight clicking noise as I repositioned it on the rest.

The buck whirled around just as I muscled the bow back to full draw. My arms were quivering from the cold and strain, and I know my anchor point was less than perfect. The eight-pointer was nearly broadside but quartering away slightly, and my release was a bummer.

I missed the buck clean, and never saw him again.

Lessons here? Sure. The biggest lesson is to practice drawing from a sitting position. Different muscles are used, and it's awkward the first few times you do it but constant practice from a sitting position will be advantageous during hunting season.

The second lesson I learned that day was to crank my bow down a few pounds during cold weather. Practice with the new setting, and know where the arrow will hit. Heavy clothing and heavy poundage will do strange things to the human body when the weather turns cold.

Instinctive Shooting or Bowhunter Sights

The first ten years I bowhunted I shot instinctively. I looked down the arrow, over the broadhead and at my target. When it looked and felt right I turned it loose. I've never been a great target shot, but during those early years I managed to down eight bull caribou, a black bear, a wild boar and ten whitetail bucks with a bow. All were shot instinctively.

Then, it all fell apart. My eyes changed with middle age, and with that change came bifocals. Why, I couldn't hit a bull in the backside shooting instinctively. My arrows hit the top, bottom, right and left edges of the paper target—when they hit the target at all. I sprayed arrows like water from a garden hose.

It was give up bowhunting or take up using sight pins. I chose the latter, and am happy I did. The sights perked up my hits on targets, and gave me the confidence I needed to hunt big game again.

There are many oldtimers who still shoot instinctively, and they scoff at sight shooters. Big deal. All I know is that sight pins have kept me bowhunting, and that's a plus factor for me.

A beginning bowhunter of 35 years or under will almost always start out shooting instinctively. As we pass over the hill into middle age it does strange things to our eyesight, and sights become somewhat easier to use. I advocate instinctive shooting when-

Claude Pollington is a better than average instinctive shooter. He adjusts his finger tabs before going out hunting.

ever and wherever possible, but for those whose eyes have taken a downhill turn sight pins are a possible cure for poor shooting.

Sight pins come in many different forms. Some are pins, others have fluorescent pink or red rings of varying sizes to be used at different distances, some have crosshairs like rifle scopes and others are lighted pins. I've tried them all and favor the lighted sight pins because much of my hunting (and shooting) at whitetail deer takes place during the low-light periods of dawn and dusk.

I favor yellow or red lighted pins, and the smaller the lighted area the better. Sportronics of Detroit makes a good lighted pin, as does Cobra and Logan. Countless companies produce unlighted pins or sights. Fine-Line, Chek-It, Bear, Browning, Martin Tru-Shot, Bowscope, Fisher, Altier, Range-O-Matic, PSE and Zero Peep Sight are several I've used or have seen used by hunting friends.

Instinctive or sights. It's as personal as the color of socks you'll wear tomorrow. Give them a try, and decide for yourself.

Bowhunter Clothing

Clothes make the man, as the saying goes, and the same holds true for bowhunters. Good clothing is important, and since bowhunters do their thing in camouflage it pays to purchase quality clothes which will hold up to trek after trek through briers, brambles and shinnying up and down trees.

I'm sold on wool. It's warm during cold weather or when wet, and it's quiet. Granted, down clothing also is warm, but most manufacturers produce down garments in a nylon shell. The stuff makes more noise than a two-year-old playing with a box of Corn Flakes, and so help me I can't sit quietly while wearing down outer garments.

One company stands head and shoulders over all others in the production of wool camo clothing suitable for bowhunters. King Of The Mountain Sports, Inc., Box 1151, Novato, CA 94948, produces quality shirts and pants in several color patterns. The workmanship is superb, and the high prices are justified.

Several companies produce wool or wool-acrylic blended garments. These serve the purpose well if worn as outer garments. The whole secret of quiet movement once a buck approaches within bow range is to wear clothing that will not scratch or make noises as the bow arm is extended and the hunter comes to full draw. Nylon, cotton and synthetics materials fail this test.

Camouflage clothing comes in a variety of color combinations and patterns. Choose the correct pattern and color for the season. Use green and brown early in most areas, brown and black after the leaf drop occurs and brown, white and/or brown-white once snow falls.

Choose the quietest outer clothing you can find or afford to buy. This means shirts, jackets, sweaters, vests, pants and hat.

My normal mild-weather bowhunting uniform consists of: blue jeans, one pair cotton and one pair wool socks, a brown or camo chamois cloth shirt, green wool stag pants and a camo wool sweater. My choice of bowhunting footwear is a pair of knee-high rubber boots, and I tuck jeans and wool pants into my boots to avoid leaving human scent as I walk into the hunting area. I wear suspenders; belts squeak. A pair of brown jersey gloves cover my hands and wrists, and I use a well washed and floppy Jones-style hat. I retired my old hunting hat after twenty-five years some time ago and replaced it with another after doing a bit of cosmetic surgery on the brim. I removed the cardboard liner from the right side of the brim (over my right eye as I'm right handed) and sewed up the brim. Now, when I come to full draw the bow string doesn't push my hat brim back and I never unconsciously ease my bowstring forward away from the brim. The brim now folds up under bowstring pressure, and I wear my hat low over my eyes.

This bowhunter is dressed for mild weather—jeans, cotton and wool socks, chamois cloth shirt and rubber boots. She's checking an apple tree for whitetail activity in the area.

Tink Nathan of Safariland Hunting Corporation is dressed for winter bowhunting in Trebark camouflage clothing.

Cold-weather bowhunting is another story. I wear long johns (sometimes two pair if it's really cold), insulated (thermal) underwear top and bottom, one pair of cotton and two pair of wool stockings, my wool stag pants and rubber boots on the lower level. My trunk wears the long underwear, thermals, a down vest under a heavy chamois cloth or wool shirt, a wool camo sweater and a green-black wool jacket. A wool scarf is wrapped about my face and neck to prevent heat loss, and it serves as effective camouflage, too.

A wool stocking cap pulled low over my forehead and ears prevents valuable heat loss from my head in cold weather, and it helps camouflage the face. Wool gloves worn over cotton jersey gloves keep your hands reasonably warm, but I usually sit with my hands inside the pockets of the wool stag pants.

Handwarmers (I hate the things) can be beneficial during cold days in a ground blind or treestand. They make more sense for the treestand hunter because nimble fingers are an asset when climbing down from a tree. Too many injuries have occurred in cold weather because the hunter has relied on his fingers to grip steps or tree limbs securely, and the strength just is not there once these extremeties turn cold.

Bowhunting Accessories

Bowhunters are as gadget crazy as trout fishermen. We see something new, and we have to have it. It's not that these items aren't needed or do not have practical applications, it's just that many of us complicate our hunting with gadgets.

However, there are certain items that come under the heading of "must-haves." One of my must-haves is a tiny packsack. In it I carry a rope to drag out my deer and plastic bags for the heart and liver. It also holds a hunting knife, binoculars, small limb saw, a compass, first-aid kit, extra gloves, scents, camo makeup, face mask, a plastic box with sharpened broadheads and razor inserts, and a host of other things I discover once a year when the pack falls from a limb to the ground.

The bag would invariably fall once I was firmly ensconced on my elevated platform, and it would hit with such impact (it weighs nearly 10 pounds) that my little treasures would be scattered for 10 feet in all directions. Now I take out what is needed at the time, and leave the dumb thing on the ground where it seemingly wants to be.

Other items or accessories bowhunters need (or feel they need) are such things as cable guards to separate the cables on compound bows. Some work well, and others do not, and I don't have one on my bow.

I do have Cat Whiskers (silencers) at each end of my bow string, and Muffs on my cables to quiet the drawing of my bow once a buck enters my shooting zone. I cover the inside portion of my bow above the arrow rest with stickum-backed brown carpeting to silence the bow even more, and I have installed a Quik Lok to hold my arrow in position on the arrow rest until it comes time to shoot.

Tink Nathan is shown using a release called the Trophy Hunter by Pro Release.

One could go crazy just deciding which arrow rest to use. Look at any archery catalog, and you'll find two or three dozen of the little jaspers staring out and begging for a ride home. Talk to several hunting buddies, obtain a consensus of opinion and have the rest of your choice installed. I do recommend a hunting-type Burger Button (cushion plunger) to be installed as it can help achieve better accuracy by correcting arrow warp and flight after release.

Hunting releases or finger tabs, shooting gloves or bare fingers; I know people who kill deer each year and use one or the other. The choice is as personal as fingerprints. I use a release called The Trophy Hunter by Pro Release. Its unique ballbearing release and fingerless draw make it sure, smooth and safe.

There are a number of bow quivers on the market even though a few hunters still favor the Indian-type back quiver. I favor a removable bow quiver, and the Quikee Quiver is my favorite. It holds six arrows (all any bowhunter need carry), and it is removable within seconds. I tie a tiny piece of rawhide to the quiver with a loop in the free end and hang it off a tree limb out of my way. I do not hunt, or take shots, with the quiver in place although I know many hunters who do.

I'm always reluctant to advise hunters to carry binoculars. Many places where fringeland deer are found offer few advantages for the binocular-toting hunter. And the motion of lifting binoculars to the eyes and/or focusing the glasses can spook incoming deer.

However, binoculars serve a useful function in certain fringeland areas. They allow the sportsman to glass an animal long before it approaches bow range, and it helps bowmen to determine the antler size if they trophy hunt. I've found binoculars useful to check an area 200 yards away before walking through it, and glasses have come in handy for watching a deer crossing from an elevated platform or ground level blind. I have two pair: a set of 8 X 40s and a small set of compact binoculars which I use from treestands.

One of the most useful items any bowhunter can attach to his bow is a Game Tracker. This string tracker attaches a 17-pound line directly behind the broadhead, and when the arrow strikes a deer the line peels off and gives the hunter an easy means of following his animal. Every bowhunter would be wise to use a Game Tracker at all times.

When to Shoot, Where to Aim

There isn't a bowhunter worth his camo clothing who doesn't dream of seeing a buck in the standard calendar pose. You know the scene: a buck standing broadside to the camera with nostrils quivering and every sense alert. The bowman just knows he could thump that animal and collect the prize of a lifetime.

Paul Jalon uses a Game Tracker to follow up any deer he shoots with a bow. This string tracker has helped many bowhunters recover a buck that otherwise would have been lost. Below, he attaches the string to his broadhead.

I've killed a number of whitetails with a bow, and so have my close hunting buddies. To a man, we regard the calendar pose as poppycock. Standing deer are tough to shoot! If you don't think so take another look at the photo. The deer's muscles often are bunched, every nerve end is jangling and the animal is ready to bolt. What do you think will happen when you come to full draw and the arrow whispers off the rest when you make a release?

Do you think the buck will stand rooted in one spot and wait for destiny to overtake him? I doubt it.

You've heard of deer "jumping the string," i.e., moving when they heard the string go forward as it releases the arrow. Well, it's true; whitetails do jump the string, and their reflexes are so sharp that only bad hits are made and it often means a complete arrow miss.

It's difficult to counsel others on when to shoot or where to aim. Claude Pollington, a man with hundreds of deer on his spread and countless bucks to his credit, detests a standing target. His reasoning is simple.

"A moving buck is making noise," Pollington says. "It makes noise as it walks, as it feeds and whenever it moves. A walking deer is frankly easier to hit than a standing animal."

Pollington advises bowhunters to wait for their shot. He likes to take his shot after the buck passes his stand and is moving slightly away. A quartering away shot allows the arrow to slide up through the soft belly behind the ribs and into the engine compartment.

"A quartering away shot is deadly," he states. "The next best shot is a broadside shot as the buck moves across in front of your blind. The worst shot is a head-on or tail-on shot, and I'll pass them up every time in hopes something better presents itself."

Picking your shot means watching deer, and knowing what they will do at any given moment. This comes from experience. It means watching their head, and being able to time their movements so you know when the head will come up to study nearby terrain. It also means watching other nearby deer; one wrong move when other animals are within range, and the object of your arrow may soon disappear over the nearest ridge because other deer happen to spook your target.

I like to make my draw when a buck has his head down feeding or is following the scent trail of an in-season doe. Keep your movements slow, and do not be afraid to stop in mid-draw. I've sat for long minutes with bow arm extended when a deer caught my movement, and then shot the animal after it decided it wasn't alarmed. I'd complete my draw once the animal's head went back down to feed.

Be aware of a key whitetail trait. They often put head fakes on hunters like a basketball player trying to juke out an opponent. They lower their head when suspicious, and abruptly raise it again in hopes of spotting some movement. Let a buck do this once or twice, and he'll soon tire of trying to spot movement and give you time to draw.

Years ago an old bowhunter gave me a piece of advice I've followed to this day. I practice it often, and it pays off with buck venison.

"Draw down on every deer that passes within range," he told me. "Pretend you will shoot every deer (buck or doe) within range. You'll soon learn when to draw on the animal and where to hold. You'll hold life and death in your hands. Within one season you could easily shoot every deer within bow range if you wanted, and this experience will be invaluable when it does come time to loose an arrow."

I've followed this philosophy, and each year will pass up at least two dozen whitetail bucks and does that could be shot. I seldom shoot early in the bow season because I enjoy bowhunting so much I don't want it to end, and that means countless deer pass my stand each year. There's not a one that goes by I don't ease back to full draw on, · and amazingly enough, only about once each season will a whitetail spot any movement and spook. Most of the time I have deer dead to rights, and choose to pass up the shot. It's great practice.

Where to shoot is a dicey question. It depends on the degree of archery skill possessed by each bowman, and it also depends on the type of shot you prefer. I favor the heart-lung shot low behind the shoulder, and this shot is preferred by most bowhunters. The liver shot slightly farther back is deadly, but a near miss means a hit in the paunch and a long tracking job after a suffering animal. I never take neck shots with a bow because the chance of wounding is too great, and head-on shots are easily deflected. The same goes for hind-end-to shots or a shot at the rear leg and its femoral artery.

The heart-lung shot is deadly. A good hit in this area will drop most deer within 100 yards, and the blood trail (if you're not using a Game Tracker) is bold and bright. Claude Pollington sums it up as well as anyone I know.

He says: "Wait for the shot you want. Settle for the heart-lung area, and pass up everything else. If you haven't got a shot at this vital area wait and perhaps the animal will turn and provide you with the desired target. Don't get antsy and just shoot at the deer but pick a precise target. Knuckle down on the area you want to hit, and settle for nothing less.

"Get a firm anchor, and make a smooth release when the deer delivers the right shot. Make a mental note of where the arrow hit, and give the deer at last fifteen minutes before following the blood trail. Listen hard immediately after the shot, and many times you'll hear the deer fall. You should be able to walk right to a bow-shot deer if all your senses are attuned to the hunt."

Scents or Non-Scents

Do deer scents work? And, if so, why?

Two good questions, and I'm not sure I know the complete answer although I've spent years studying the effects of cover-up, food or sex scents on whitetails. All I know is two of the three work for me, and I'm convinced that with the proper application they can work for you.

There is nothing guaranteed when hunting whitetail deer. The animals react differently in certain areas, and a scent may work in one place and a similar scent may spook deer in another. I'm convinced the reason scents fail to produce for some hunters is because of some human error. A hunter may lay down a human scent trail, the wind may switch and place the hunter upwind of approaching deer or it may just be sloppiness in placing the scent that foils a bowman's attempt to use a scent.

I've stated elsewhere in this book that I've had no success with food scents. I've had good success with masking scents (such as skunk or fox), and better than average results with sex scents.

Let's consider a place I hunt often. Adapt the following procedures to your hunting locale, and you should be in business.

I circle far around downwind from my selected hunting site, and then walk upwind into my area. Once I'm 25–30 yards downwind from my blind I'll fill two or three cotton-filled 35mm film canisters with skunk scent and place them in a semicircle downwind of my blind or stand. I'll walk into the area with pads on my feet which have been saturated with skunk or sex scent, and this (along with my knee-high rubber boots) seems to kill any human scent providing I use caution not to brush against trees or brush with my upper body.

Saturate pads with skunk scent or a deer sex scent before walking into a hunting area. This can kill or neutralize any human scent.

Dave Richey, Jr. fills empty 35mm film cannisters with clean cotton and saturates it with a good sex scent.

A line-up of three good sex or masking scents.

178

Upwind 10 to 25 yards from my stand or blind, where I expect a buck to appear, I'll place one, two or three cotton-filled 35mm film canisters laced with a good sex scent. Any buck which enters the area will probably catch a whiff of a doe whitetail in heat, and will come to investigate the odor. These sex-scent-filled canisters are placed where I want the buck to stop. If the animal stops to smell one or more canisters, I'll have ample opportunity for a shot.

Last year I took Ruth Ann Pollington's treestand. She had hunted daily for three weeks, and decided not to go out one evening. She offered me her stand, and I took it.

I walked into the area, placed my masking scent containers downwind of the tree-stand and my sex-scent canisters where I wanted a buck to stop. Thirty minutes later a buck walked out from the swamp, stopped to sniff the sex scent, and I shot him.

It was as easy as that.

Too much skunk or fox scent will ruin your chances, and too little sex scent will do the same. Experiment with each, and follow the directions issued with each scent.

I've used a raft of different products containing scent, and here are the results of my tests. They may not be conclusive, but the tests did prove the following things about these products to me.

BIGAME PRODUCTS, INC., 20551 Sunset Avenue, Detroit, MI 48234. A manufacturer of neutral and olive-drab camouflage-painted scent lures. I've used this product,

Good camouflage is important for bow-hunters. Kathy Marchetta applies hers before a car mirror.

and feel it has exciting possibilities. It offers a scent which will help mask human odor while enabling the hunter to use the olive-drab product to camouflage exposed skin.

BUCK STIX, PO Box 3, Neenah, WI 54956. The producer has made a pen-type product designed to release through vapor action an apple, pine, doe-in-heat or musk scent. I've used the musk scent, but not the others. A novel idea.

Bigame Camouflage Creme is available in a variety of scents.

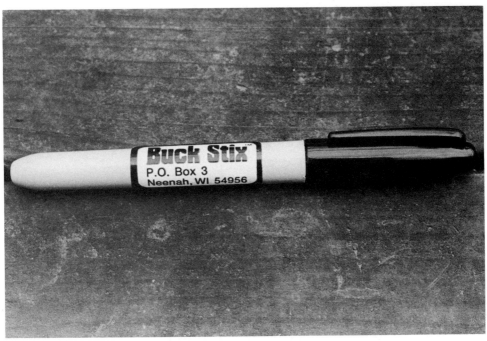

Buck Stix is a pen-type dispenser of skunk scent which can mask your odor.

DESIGN IDEAS, PO Box 37293, Cincinnati, OH 45222. This company has produced the Puff Bottle, a wind-direction powder that can be squeezed to check wind direction. It's available in acorn, apple, cedar, pine and unscented. It's a great hunter aid.

FOX TRAIL, 3711 E. 106th Street, Chicago, IL 60617. The producer of Fox Trail, a masking agent to cover human odor. It seems to work although I haven't shot a deer while using it. I'll continue to test it on future hunts.

PETE RICKARD, INC., Cobleskill, NY 12043. The producer of Super Doe Buck Lure, Original Indian Buck Lure, Natural Skunk Essence, Fox Scent Formula, Apple-X Deer Lure, Alpine Scent, Acorn Deer Lure and Cedar Scent. I've shot bucks while using the Original Indian Buck Lure, and this product is used by many bowhunters.

SAFARILAND HUNTING CORPORATION, PO Box NN, McLean, VA 22101. They produce Tink's #69 Doe-In-Rut Buck Lure, Tink's #1 Doe-P Deer Scent, Tink's #2 Dixie Deer Scent, Tink's Non-Scent Internal Camouflage Tablets, Tink's Stink Skunk Scent #10, Tink's Red Fox-P Cover Scent and Tink's Vixen Cover Scent. I've used all products listed and prefer the Doe-In-Rut and Doe-P over all other sex lures tried. The Stink Skunk Scent and Red Fox-P are both excellent masking scents.

SKUNK SKREEN, 315 Church Street, College Station, TX 77841. Tex Isbell's products include Skunk Skreen and Buck-N-Mate. I've used the masking liquids, which must be mixed, and they seem to negate human odor.

Tink's Non Scent chlorophyll tablets to reduce human odor.

Tink's Dixie Deer Scent #2 and Tink's #1 Doe-P sex scents.

SKUNKS UNLIMITED, Route 4, Box 85, Cumberland, WI 54829. This company produces Nature's Way Super Skunk liquid, Super Skunk Spray and Fox Camo Scent. I've used all products, and feel the spray has excellent hunter potential. The Super Skunk liquid is potent. I've watched whitetail bucks and does circle downwind without catching my scent.

CHAPTER 10

State-By-State Fringeland Deer Report

A state-by-state or province-by-province report on the status of fringeland deer is a nebulous thing at best. The very nature of habitat where fringeland whitetails are found can and will change from one growing season to another.

Factors such as hunting pressure, changing farming practices and even game management policies can alter the information contained in this chapter. This chapter is meant to be a beginner's guide to each state, and is not meant to be the final word on where to hunt. Keep your eyes and ears open at all times, and study deer in your area. Use this data only as a basis for starting your own campaign to learn more about local deer.

ALABAMA

Number of deer hunters annually—207,981

Whitetail harvest in last known year—151,477 (1983)

Status of whitetail deer herd—Stable

Percentage of state land open to hunting is fringeland—20%

Which areas hold most promise for fringeland deer hunters—Blackbelt (southcentral part of state)

Best counties for trophy bucks—Macon, Bullock, Montgomery, Lowndes, Wilcox, Dallas, Marengo, Hale, Perry and Tuscaloosa.

Favorite agricultural and wild foods for fringeland whitetails—Soybeans, wheat, acorns, honeysuckle, greenbrier, dogwood, blackberry and sumac.

Address for more information—Wildlife Section, Alabama Game & Fish Division, 64 North Union Street, Montgomery, AL 36130.

ALASKA

Did not respond.

ARIZONA

Number of deer hunters annually—20,000

Whitetail harvest in last known year—4,000 (1983)

Status of whitetail deer herd—Increasing

Percentage of state land open to hunting is fringeland—Unknown

Which areas hold most promise for fringeland hunters—"Fringeland occurs in the mountainous regions of the southeastern quarter of state, and it holds the most promise for whitetail deer hunters," State of Arizona.

Best counties for trophy bucks—Cochise, Santa Cruz, Pima, Graham and Gila.

Address for more information—Arizona Game & Fish Department, 2222 W. Greenway, Phoenix, AZ 85023.

ARKANSAS

Number of deer hunters annually—257,000 (1982)

Whitetail harvest in last known year—42,873 (1982)

Status of deer herd—Stable statewide, up in some areas.

Percentage of state land open to hunting is fringeland—90%

Which areas hold most promise for fringeland deer hunters—southcentral, southeast, southwest and northcentral.

Best counties for trophy bucks—Arkansas, Prairie, Monroe, Lonoke and Woodruff.

Best deer hunting counties—Arkansas, Dallas, Union, Clark, Cleveland, Ouachita, Calhoun, Nevada, Desha, Hempstead, Bradley, Drew, Columbia, Sharp, Grant, Howard, Madison, Fulton, Sebastian, Monroe and Izard.

Address for more information—Arkansas Game & Fish Commission, Game & Fish Building, #2 Natural Resources Drive, Little Rock, AR 72205.

CALIFORNIA
No whitetail deer.

COLORADO
Number of deer hunters annually—192,000 (1982)

Whitetail harvest in last known year—Unknown

Status of whitetail deer herd—Increasing

Percentage of state land open to hunting is fringeland—"Most whitetail hunting land open is fringeland because of the nature of farm and ranch lands," State of Colorado.

Which areas hold most promise for fringeland deer hunters—South Platte River drainage in Washington and Logan counties; Republican River drainage in Yuma County; Eastern Plains.

Best counties hold most promise for fringeland deer hunters—Washington, Logan and Yuma. Weld, Adams and Elbert also good.

Best counties for trophy bucks—Unknown. No whitetail trophies measured in Colorado.

Address for more information—Colorado Division of Wildlife, 6060 Broadway, Denver, CO 80216.

CONNECTICUT
Did not respond.

DELAWARE
Number of deer hunters annually—15,000

Whitetail harvest in last known year—2,300 (1983)

Status of deer herd—Increasing

Percentage of state land open to hunting is fringeland—70%

Which areas hold most promise for fringeland deer hunters—Coastal marsh edges and woodland-field edges

Best counties for trophy bucks—Sussex

Best counties year after year—Western Kent and Sussex

Favorite agricultural and wild foods for fringeland whitetails—soybeans

Address for more information—Delaware Division of Fish & Wildlife, PO Box 1401, 89 Kings Highway, Dover, DE 19903.

FLORIDA
Number of deer hunters annually—166,017 (1982-83)

Whitetail harvest in last known year—64,557 (1982-83)

Status of whitetail deer herd—More or less stable

Percentage of state land open to hunting is fringeland—Unknown

Which areas hold most promise for fringeland deer hunters—Fringeland areas state-wide. Best in northeast and northwest.

Best counties for trophy bucks—Leon, Jefferson, Gadsden, Jackson and Holmes.

Favorite agricultural and wild foods for fringeland whitetails—Soybeans, corn, peas, rye and rye grass.

Address for more information—Florida Game & Freshwater Fish Commission, Division of Wildlife, 620 S. Meridian Street, Tallahassee, FL 32301.

GEORGIA

Number of deer hunters annually—242,000 licensed; 25% unlicensed

Whitetail harvest in last known year—142,000

Status of whitetail deer herd—Showing a slight increase

Percentage of state land open to hunting is fringeland—Unknown

Which areas hold most promise for fringeland deer hunters—"The Piedmont area," State of Georgia.

Best counties for trophy bucks—Western Piedmont counties and western upper coastal plains counties.

Best deer counties, year after year—Piedmont region.

Favorite agricultural and wild foods for fringeland whitetails—Soybeans, winter grains, acorns, honeysuckle, greenbrier and yellow jasmine.

Address for more information—Georgia Game Division, 270 Washington Street, Atlanta, GA 30334.

HAWAII

No whitetail deer.

IDAHO

Number of deer hunters annually—120,809 (includes mule deer)

Whitetail harvest in last known year—10,406 (1982)

Status of whitetail deer herd—Stable

Percentage of state land open to hunting is fringeland—75%

Which areas hold most promise for fringeland deer hunters—"North Idaho mountain valleys," State of Idaho.

Best counties for trophy bucks—Regions 1 and 2, units 1, 2, 3, 4, 5, 6, 8 and 8A

Best counties for whitetail deer, year after year—Same as above

Address for more information—Wildlife Division, Fish & Game Department, Box 25, Boise, ID 83707.

ILLINOIS

Number of deer hunters annually—82,000

Whitetail harvest in last known year—Unknown

Status of whitetail deer herd—Increasing

Percentage of state land open to hunting is fringeland—95%

Which areas hold most promise for fringeland deer hunters—"The Mississippi and Illinois river valleys from St. Louis, Missouri north to the Wisconsin line. West Central area between the two rivers has increased kills yearly," State of Illinois.

Best counties for trophy bucks—Adams, Carroll, Jo Daviess, Hancock, Hardin, Pike and Pope. Try northeastern counties near Chicago with bow-arrow as they are closed to firearms.

Address for more information—Illinois Department of Conservation, Wildlife Division, 524 South Second Street, Springfield, IL 62706.

INDIANA

Number of deer hunters annually—180,000

Whitetail harvest in last known year—25,232 (1983)

Status of whitetail deer herd—Increasing

Percentage of state land open to hunting is fringeland—16 million acres cropland or pasture; 3.5 million acres are forested.

Which areas hold most promise for fringeland deer hunters—Southcentral (Zone 6) and northeast (Zone 1).

Best counties for trophy bucks—Pike, Warrick, Spencer, Sullivan, Perry, Jefferson, Switzerland, Martin and Crawford.

Best area for deer hunters, year after year—Zone 6

Address for more information—Division of Fish & Wildlife, 607 State Office Building, Indianapolis, IN 46204.

IOWA

Number of deer hunters annually—110,000

Whitetail harvest in last known year—26,000 (1982)

Status of whitetail deer herd—Increasing

Percentage of state land open to hunting is fringeland—100%

Which areas hold most promise for fringeland deer hunters—"Southern Iowa, but basically statewide," State of Iowa.

Best counties for trophy bucks—Statewide.

Best areas in state for deer hunters, year after year—Southeast, southwest and northeast areas.

Address for more information—Fish & Wildlife Division, Iowa Conservation Commission, Wallace Office Building, Des Moines, IA 50319

KANSAS

Number of deer hunters annually—38,924 (1983)

Whitetail harvest in last known year—10,130 (1982)

Status of whitetail deer herd—Increasing

Percentage of state land open to hunting is fringeland—95%

Which areas hold most promise for fringeland deer hunters—"Any of our public areas in the eastern half of Kansas would provide good fringeland deer hunting," State of Kansas.

Best counties for trophy bucks—Eastern two-thirds of state provide best whitetails.

Best area in state for deer, year after year—Eastern one-third provides excellent whitetail hunting.

Address for more information—Kansas Fish & Game, RR 2, Box 54A, Pratt, KS 67124.

KENTUCKY

Number of deer hunters annually—140,000

Whitetail harvest in last known year—Estimated 25,000

Status of whitetail deer herd—Increasing

Percentage of state land open to hunting is fringeland—All except for heavily forested regions in eastern Kentucky mountains.

Which areas hold most promise for fringeland deer hunters—Northcentral and west-central parts of state.

Best counties for trophy bucks—Northcentral and west-central.

Best areas for deer hunters, year after year—Same areas.

Favorite agricultural and wild foods for fringeland whitetails—Soybeans, clover, alfalfa, greenbrier and most second-growth plants.

Address for more information—Fish & Wildlife, #1 Game Farm Road, Frankfort, KY 040601.

LOUISIANA

Number of deer hunters annually—Unknown.

Whitetail harvest in last known year—132,000 (1983)

Status of whitetail deer herd—Static.

Percentage of state land open to hunting is fringeland—60%

Which areas hold most promise for fringeland deer hunters—North, northwest and northcentral parishes (counties).

Best counties for deer hunters, year after year—Winn, Brenville, Union, Jackson, Grant, Claiborne, DeSoto and Natchitoches for open hunting. East Carrol, Madison, Tensas, Concordia and Pt. Coupee for "lease fee" controlled hunting.

Best counties for trophy bucks—East Feliciana, West Feliciana, St. Landry, Catahoula, LaSalle, Vernon, Claiborne, Bienville and DeSoto.

Address for more information—Fisheries & Game Division, PO Box 15570, Baton Rouge, LA 70895.

MAINE

Did not respond.

MARYLAND
Did not respond.

MASSACHUSETTS
Number of deer hunters annually—70,000–80,000
Whitetail harvest in last known year—4,523
Status of whitetail deer herd—Increasing
Percentage of state land open to hunting is fringeland—Unknown
Best counties for trophy bucks—Four western counties.
Best counties for hunters, year after year—Four western counties.
Favorite agricultural and wild foods for fringeland whitetails—Striped maple, black-
    berry, mushrooms, grasses and clovers.
Address for more information—Massachusetts Division of Fish & Wildlife, Field Head-
    quarters, Westboro, MA 01581.

MICHIGAN
Number of deer hunters annually—800,000+
Whitetail harvest in last known year—154,000 (1983)
Status of whitetail deer herd—Decreasing slightly
Percentage of state land open to hunting is fringeland—25–50%
Best counties for deer hunters, year after year—Dickinson, Menominee, Montmorency,
    Oscoda, Alcona, Iosco, Ogemaw, Roscommon, Lake, Osceola, Clare, Gladwin,
    Arenac, Mecosta, Montcalm and Barry.
Best counties for trophy bucks—Ontonagon, Iron, Marquette, Delta, Schoolcraft,
    Mackinac, Ionia, Livingston, Jackson, Washtenaw and Hillsdale.
Address for more information—Michigan Department of Natural Resources, Wildlife
    Division, PO Box 30028, Lansing, MI 48909.

MINNESOTA
Did not respond.

MISSISSIPPI
Number of deer hunters annually—170,000
Whitetail harvest in last known year—210,684
Status of whitetail deer herd—Stable
Percentage of state land open to hunting is fringeland—"Most"
Best areas to hunt—"We do not release this information for it seems to unduly con-
    centrate pressure," State of Mississippi.

Address for more information—Department of Wildlife Conservation, Wildlife Division, PO Box 451, Jackson, MS 39205.

MISSOURI
Number of deer hunters annually—96,000
Whitetail harvest in last known year—42,240 (1983)
Status of whitetail deer herd—Increasing
Percentage of state land open to hunting is fringeland—10%
Which areas hold most promise for hunting fringeland deer—"The most edge is found in agricultural areas, especially northeast and northcentral Missouri, but it's an area difficult to gain hunting permission in," State of Missouri.
Best counties for trophy bucks—Those of the northeast and northcentral although one of the largest bucks of all time came from St. Louis County.
Address for more information—Wildlife Division, Missouri Department of Conservation, Box 180, Jefferson City, MO 65102

MONTANA
Number of deer hunters annually—158,521 (1982)
Whitetail harvest in last known year—27,456 (1982)
Status of whitetail deer herd—Increased in 1983
Percentage of state land open to hunting is fringeland—Unknown
Which areas hold most promise for fringeland deer hunters—In major river bottoms east of the Continental Divide.
Best counties for deer hunters, year after year—those along Missouri River.
Best counties for trophy bucks—Missoula, Flathead, Valley and Cascade.
  Other hunts—Backcountry Areas September 15–November 25
Address for more information—Montana Department of Fish, Wildlife & Parks, Wildlife Division, 1420 East 6th Avenue, Helena, MT 59620.

NEBRASKA
Did not respond.

NEVADA
No whitetail deer in Nevada.

NEW HAMPSHIRE
Number of deer hunters annually—86,000
Whitetail harvest in last known year—3,280 (1983)
Status of whitetail deer herd—Near a 50-year low.

Percentage of state land open to hunting is fringeland—50%
Which areas hold most promise for fringeland deer hunters—Farms and orchards in
    southern New Hampshire
Best counties for deer hunters, year after year—Carroll County and Lakes Region
Best counties for trophy bucks—Grafton and Carroll counties
Favorite agricultural and wild foods for fringeland whitetails—Apples, acorns, alfalfa,
    fern buds.
Address for more information—New Hampshire Department of Conservation, 34
    Bridge Street, Concord, NH 03301.

NEW JERSEY
Number of deer hunters annually—122,000
Whitetail harvest in last known year—23,000+
Status of whitetail deer herd—Stable statewide.
Percentage of state land open to hunting is fringeland—Little
Which areas hold most promise for fringeland deer hunters—Hunterdon, Middlesex,
    Mercer and Somerset.
Best counties for deer hunters, year after year—Hunterdon, Warren and Sussex.
Best counties for trophy bucks—Hunterdon, Salem, Monmouth, Mercer and northern
    Burlington.
Favorite agricultural and wild foods for fringeland whitetails—Corn and soybeans.
Address for more information—Division of Fish, Game & Wildlife, Wildlife Division,
    CN 400, Trenton, NJ 08625.

NEW MEXICO
Number of deer hunters annually—110,000
Whitetail harvest in last known year—27,133 (1982)
Status of deer herd—Stable
Percentage of state land open to hunting is fringeland—None
Best counties for trophy bucks—None
Best counties for deer hunters, year after year—New Mexico isn't known for whitetail
    deer hunting.
Address for more information—New Mexico Department of Game & Fish, Villagra
    Building, Santa Fe, NM 87503.

NEW YORK
Number of deer hunters annually—770,000
Whitetail harvest in last known year—185,455 (1982)
Status of whitetail deer herd—Gradual decline by design.
Percentage of state land open to hunting is fringeland—Unknown
Which areas hold most promise for fringeland deer hunters—All of southern zone ex-
    cept for Catskill Park.

Best counties for deer hunters, —Delaware, Steuben, Allegany and Cattaraugus.

Best counties for trophy bucks—Allegany, Steuben, Genesee, Cattaraugus, Essex, Hamilton and St. Lawrence.

Favorite agricultural and wild foods for fringeland whitetails—Alfalfa, clover, corn, apple, mountain maple, striped maple, red maple, witch hobble, basswood, wintergreen and dogwood.

Address for more information—New York State Department of Environmental Conservation, Wildlife Center, Delmar, NY 12054.

NORTH CAROLINA

Number of deer hunters annually—270,000

Whitetail harvest in last known year—47,646

Status of whitetail deer herd—Slightly increasing

Percentage of state land open to hunting is fringeland—Unknown

Which areas hold most promise for fringeland deer hunters—Piedmont and Upper Coastal Plains.

Best counties for deer hunters, year after year—Coastal Plains Region

Best counties for trophy bucks—Piedmont Region

Favorite agricultural and wild foods for fringeland whitetails—Corn, soybeans, peanuts, wheat, rye, acorn mast, hardwood browse.

Contact Division of Wilderness Management, 512 Salisbury, Raleigh, NC 27611.

NORTH DAKOTA

Number of deer hunters annually—55,000-60,000

Whitetail harvest in last known year—32,210 (1982)

Status of whitetail deer herd—Increasing

Percentage of state land open to hunting is fringeland—80%

Which areas hold most promise for fringeland deer hunters—Extreme northeast, southcentral and extreme southwest

Best counties for deer hunters, year after year—Slope, Bowman, McIntosh and Cavalier.

Best counties for trophy bucks—None in particular.

Address for more information—North Dakota Game & Fish Commission, 2121 Lovett Avenue, Bismarck, ND 58505.

OHIO

Number of deer hunters annually—250,000 to 300,000

Whitetail harvest in last known year—52,885 (1982)

Status of whitetail deer herd—Increasing slightly.

Percentage of state land open to hunting is fringeland—Whole state.

Which areas hold most promise for fringeland deer hunters—Unglaciated region of eastern Ohio known as the Hill Country.

Best counties for deer hunters, year after year—Counties in the Hill Country.

Best counties for trophy bucks—Most big bucks come from the Hill County of eastern Ohio.

Address for more information—Ohio Department of Natural Resources, Division of Wildlife, Fountain Square Building C, Columbus, OH 43224.

OKLAHOMA

Number of deer hunters annually—190,130

Whitetail harvest in last known year—21,600+

Status of whitetail deer herd—Increasing.

Percentage of state land open to hunting is fringeland—90%

Which areas hold most promise for fringeland deer hunters—Cultivated small grains.

Best counties for hunting, year after year—Osage, Washington, Nowata, Rogers, Craig, Pittsburg, Ottawa, LeFlore and McCurtain.

Best counties for trophy bucks—Harper, Woods, Ellis, Latimer, McCurtain and LeFlore.

Favorite agricultural and wild foods for fringeland whitetails—Alfalfa, corn, wheat, soybeans, mung beans, acorns.

Address for more information—Oklahoma Department of Wildlife Conservation, 1801 N. Lincoln, Oklahoma City, OK 73105.

OREGON

Only a few whitetails taken each year.

PENNSYLVANIA

Number of deer hunters annually—950,000

Whitetail harvest in last known year—138,222 (1982)

Status of whitetail deer herd—Decreasing statewide

Percentage of state land open to hunting is fringeland—Unknown

Which areas hold most promise for fringeland deer hunters—Southcentral area.

Best counties for deer hunters, year after year—Statewide where land access is available.

Best counties for trophy bucks—Southeast Pennsylvania where access is most difficult.

Address for more information—Pennsylvania Game Commission, Box 1567, Harrisburg, PA 17120.

RHODE ISLAND

Number of deer hunters annually—4,805

Whitetail harvest in last known year—205

Status of whitetail deer herd—Stable

Percentage of state land open to hunting is fringeland—30% fringeland—70% forest land.

Which areas hold most promise for fringeland deer hunters—Washington County.

Best areas for deer hunters, year after year—Near towns of Exeter and West Greenwich.

Best counties for trophy bucks—Not applicable in Rhode Island.

Address for more information—Rhode Island Fish & Wildlife, Box 218, W. Kingston, RI 02892.

SOUTH CAROLINA
Did not respond.

SOUTH DAKOTA
Number of deer hunters annually—64,000

Whitetail harvest in last known year—29,000

Status of whitetail deer herd—Increasing

Percentage of state land open to hunting is fringeland—80–90 percent of 175,000 acres of public land east of the Missouri River.

Which areas hold most promise for fringeland deer hunters—"East of the Missouri River. Try West River and the foothills off the Black Hills and wooded river bottoms," State of South Dakota.

Which counties are best for deer hunters, year after year—Brown, Clark, Day, Spink and Marshall. Nonresidents only allowed to hunt this area with bow.

Which counties are best for trophy bucks—Try Brown, Clark, Marshall and Spink.

Address for more information—445 E. Capitol, Pierre, SD 57501.

TENNESSEE
Number of deer hunters annually—170,000

Whitetail harvest in last known year—40,370

Status of whitetail deer herd—Increasing

Percentage of state land open to hunting is fringeland—40%

Which areas hold most promise for fringeland deer hunters—Western half of state.

Best counties for deer hunters, year after year—Giles, Hardeman, Henry, Hickman, Humphreys and McNairy.

Best counties for trophy bucks—Montgomery.

Favorite agricultural and wild foods for fringeland whitetails—Acorns, corn, honeysuckle, soybeans and winter wheat.

Address for more information—Department of Wildlife Conservation, Box 40747, Nashville, TN 37204.

TEXAS
Number of deer hunters annually—525,000

Whitetail harvest in last known year—337,621 (1982)

Status of whitetail deer herd—Static at 3,250,000

Percentage of state land open to hunting is fringeland—10–15%

Which areas hold most promise for fringeland deer hunters—Rolling plains, piney woods, Transpecos, Gulf Prairies.

Which counties are best for hunters, year after year—West of Pecos River and Rolling Plains.

Best counties for trophy bucks—Rolling Plains.

Favorite agricultural and wild foods for fringeland whitetails—Milo, soybeans, corn, oats, cactus, mesquite beans, post oak acorns.

Address for more information—Texas Parks & Wildlife, 4200 Smith School Road, Austin, TX 78744.

UTAH
No free-roaming whitetails.

VERMONT
Number of deer hunters annually—126,793 (1982)

Whitetail harvest in last known year—6,630 (1983)

Status of whitetail deer herd—Stable. Slight 1983 increase.

Percentage of state land open to hunting is fringeland—"Most"

Which areas hold most promise for fringeland deer hunters—"83 percent of Vermont is forested. Area along Lake Champlain offers the most open land," State of Vermont.

Best counties for deer hunting, year after year—Bennington, Rutland, Windham and Windsor.

Best counties for trophy bucks—Caledonia and Essex counties.

Favorite agricultural and wild foods for fringeland whitetails—Corn, winter wheat, winter rye, apples, raspberries, blackberries.

Address for more information—Fish & Game Department, Information-Education, Montpelier, VT 05602.

VIRGINIA
Number of deer hunters annually—288,737

Whitetail harvest in last known year—88,745 (1982)

Status of whitetail deer herd—Increasing

Percentage of state land open to hunting is fringeland—35%

Which areas hold most promise for fringeland deer hunters—"Eastern management areas located in agricultural sections; edges of National Forest bordering agricultural lands," State of Virginia.

Best counties for deer hunters, year after year—Bath, Bedford, Buckingham, Carolina, Granson, Rockingham, Shenandoah and Southampton.

Best counties for trophy bucks—Augusta, Bath, Grayson, Rockingham, Shenandoah, and counties along east slope of the Blue Ridge Mountains.

Favorite agricultural and wild foods for fringeland deer—Alfalfa, apples, corn, garden vegetables, grass, soybeans.

Address for more information—Virginia Game Commission, Box 11104, Richmond, VA 23230.

WASHINGTON
Number of deer hunters annually—200,000

Whitetail harvest in last known year—7,400

Status of whitetail deer herd—Stable

Percentage of state land open to hunting is fringeland—Unknown

Which areas hold most promise for fringeland deer hunters—"Upland areas surrounding the Blue Mountains in southeast Washington; valleys and farmlands of northeast Washington; Okanogan River Valley of northcentral Washington," State of Washington.

Best counties for deer hunters, year after year—Try northeastern Washington.

Best counties for trophy bucks—Pend Oreille and Stevens counties.

Address for more information—Washington Department of Game, Wildlife Management Division, 600 N. Capitol Way, Olympia, WA 98504.

WEST VIRGINIA

Number of deer hunters annually—243,000 (1980)

Whitetail harvest in last known year—89,840 (1983)

Status of whitetail deer herd—Increasing

Percentage of state land open to hunting is fringeland—Unknown

Which areas hold most promise for fringeland deer hunters—Central and western counties.

Best counties for deer hunters, year after year—"Northcentral counties in mountain region and western counties near Ohio River," State of West Virginia.

Best counties for trophy bucks—"Eastern mountainous counties where we have large, relatively roadless areas, and southern counties where hunting pressure is light," State of West Virginia.

Address for more information—Wildlife Resources Division, 1800 Washington Street East, Charleston, WV 25305.

WISCONSIN

Number of deer hunters annually—640,000

Whitetail harvest in last known year—220,000

Status of whitetail deer herd—Increasing

Percentage of state land open to hunting is fringeland—10%

Which areas hold most promise for fringeland deer hunters—Central and southwestern counties.

Best counties for deer hunters, year after year—Central and southwestern counties.

Best counties for trophy bucks—Northern and western counties.

Address for more information—Wisconsin Department of Natural Resources, Bureau of Wildlife Management, PO Box 7921, Madison, WI 53707.

WYOMING

Did not respond.

CANADA

ALBERTA
Did not respond.

BRITISH COLUMBIA
Did not respond.

ONTARIO
Did not respond.

QUEBEC
Number of deer hunters annually—100,000
Whitetail harvest in last known year—9,500
Status of whitetail deer herd—Increasing
Percentage of provincial land is fringeland—25%
Which areas hold most promise for fringeland deer hunters—Outaonais and Eastern townships.
Best counties for deer hunters, year after year—Hunting zones A-3 and F-2, and Anticosti Island.
Best counties for trophy bucks—Zones D-1, F-2, F-3 and F-4.
Address for more information—Ministere du Loisir, de la Chasse et de la Peche, Direction Genera; de la faimes, 150 est St-Cyrille, Quebec, QC G1R4Y1.

NEWFOUNDLAND
Whitetail deer do not exist in this province.

MANITOBA
Number of deer hunters annually—49,000
Whitetail harvest in last known year—Unknown
Status of whitetail deer herd—Stable.
Percentage of provincial land open to hunting is fringeland—Almost all.
Which areas hold most promise for fringeland deer hunters—Game Hunting Areas 22, 27 and 28.
Best counties for trophy bucks—Game Hunting Areas 22, 27, 28, 24, 25A and 25.
Favorite agricultural and wild foods for fringeland whitetails—Acorns, alfalfa, corn, fall rye, snowberry and sunflowers.
Address for more information—Wildlife Division, 1495 St. James Street, Winnipeg, Manitoba, R3H 0W9.

NOVA SCOTIA
Number of deer hunters annually—100,000

Whitetail harvest in last known year—40,000

Status of whitetail deer herd—Increasing

Percentage of provincial land open to hunting is fringeland—80 percent

Which areas hold most promise for fringeland deer hunters—Northeastern Nova Scotia.

Best areas for deer hunters, year after year—Northeastern counties.

Best areas for trophy bucks—Eastern counties.

Favorite agricultural or wild foods for fringeland whitetails—After grass, red maple shoots, and spring flora-fauna.

Address for more information—Nova Scotia Department of Lands & Forests, Wildlife Division, Kentville, NS.

SASKATCHEWAN

Number of deer hunters annually—70,606

Whitetail harvest in last known year—36,000 (1982-83)

Status of whitetail deer herd—Stable. Increases in some areas.

Percentage of provincial land open to hunting is fringeland—50 percent.

Which areas hold most promise for fringeland deer hunters—"Zones open to Canadian resident and nonresident hunters, particularly those on the east and west sides of the province," Province of Saskatchewan.

Best counties for trophy bucks—The best counties are in the fringe areas including #10. Another good bet is near Hudson Bay, Maryfield, Kandahar, Abbey, Southwest Abbey, Carrot River and Prairie River.

Address for more information—Saskatchewan Tourism & Small Business, Bank of Montreal Building, 2103 11th Avenue, Regina, Saskatchewan S4P 3V7.

PRINCE EDWARD ISLAND

No wild deer population on Island.

NORTHWEST TERRITORIES

No response.

YUKON TERRITORY

No response.

Index